D0065980

Heart Full of Grace

A THOUSAND YEARS OF BLACK WISDOM

Edited by Venice Johnson

942750

SIMON & SCHUSTER

New York   London   Sydney

Toronto   Tokyo   Singapore

Chattahoochee Co.

SIMON & SCHUSTER
Rockefeller Center
1230 Avenue of the Americas
New York, NY 10020

SIMON & SCHUSTER and colophon are registered trademarks
of Simon & Schuster Inc.

Design and art by Karolina Harris

Manufactured in the United States of America

3   5   7   9   10   8   6   4   2

Library of Congress Cataloging-in-Publication Data
Heart full of grace: a thousand years of black wisdom /
edited by Venice Johnson.
p.   cm.
Includes index.
1. Blacks—Quotations, maxims, etc.   2. Afro-Americans—
Quotations, maxims, etc.   I. Johnson, Venice.
PN6081.3.H43   1995
082'.08996—dc20   95-38106
ISBN 0-684-81428-5

Everybody can be great, because anybody can serve. . . . You only need a heart full of grace.
— MARTIN LUTHER KING, JR.

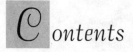

Contents

Contents

Preface

Heart Full of Grace draws on a thousand years of accumulated African and African-American wisdom. The people quoted in this book include such well-known figures as Martin Luther King, Alice Walker, and Malcolm X, as well as the anonymous voices of former slaves. There are quotations from writers, singers, athletes, and political leaders; from entrepreneurs, students, and soldiers; from the men and women who struggled to abolish slavery, took up arms in the Civil War, fought to end Jim Crow, and built the civil rights movement. We hear political speeches and manifestos, African proverbs, snatches of the blues, and even a few lines of the dozens.

Although the sayings in this book come from a wide variety of speakers, time periods, and formats, a few themes emerge with remarkable consistency. One is the theme of struggle. Throughout their long history, African-Americans have had to wrest their livelihoods from a society that consistently sought to deny them opportunity, dignity, selfhood. Perhaps ironically, this very struggle helped to forge key aspects of African-American identity: commitment to community, enormous personal determination, and great faith in the future.

Another theme that emerges is the sense of history. One of this book's sections is entitled "Heritage," and the sense of those who came before is present throughout the book.

Time and again, the people quoted speak of their personal ancestors—mothers, fathers, grandparents—as well as their communal ancestors—African griots, the leaders of slave rebellions, groundbreaking figures such as Langston Hughes and Paul Robeson. The sense that one is not fighting for oneself alone but for the entire community sustains African-Americans in a wide range of callings. The awareness of fighting not *by* oneself but as part of a continuous movement toward freedom and self-realization, likewise sustains many, if not all, of the speakers in this book.

Finally, a playful relationship to language, a humor that can be both bitter and sweet, and a pleasure in folk speech enliven many of the voices quoted here. Novelists, essayists, and poets borrow the rhythms of folk sayings and the vocabulary of the blues. Political speakers and writers adopt the majestic rhetoric of the preacher or the down-home irony of the traditional saying. The African-American cultural tradition appears in all its richness, pithy and poetic.

In *Heart Full of Grace*, you'll hear voices musing on hope and despair, on love and hate, on slavery and freedom. People will explore their dreams, share their loneliness, and reflect on the nature of unity and revolution. Welcome to the collective voice of African-Americans as they speak throughout the centuries, always seeking wisdom, often finding grace.

Venice Johnson

Heart Full of Grace

Achievement

*N*othing in the universe is attained by doing nothing. You must always give something to get something. It's extremely basic, you can't fill a cup without giving up its contents first. You can't even move to a new place in a room without giving up the space you now occupy. In other words sacrifice is a basic concept of our universe.

— AFRO-CUBAN RITE

*I*t is only what is written upon the soul of man that will survive the wreck of time.

— FRANCIS JAMES GRIMKÉ

*W*hen do any of us do enough?

— BARBARA JORDAN

We ain't what we want to be; we ain't what we gonna be; but thank God, we ain't what we was.

— AFRICAN-AMERICAN FOLK SAYING

Every man is born into the world to do something unique and something distinctive and if he or she does not do it, it will never be done.

— BENJAMIN E. MAYS

He who is not courageous enough to take risks will accomplish nothing in life.

— MUHAMMAD ALI

[T]he human race does command its own destiny and that destiny can eventually embrace the stars.

— LORRAINE HANSBERRY

Up, you mighty race, you can accomplish what you will.

— MARCUS GARVEY

*D*issatisfaction with possession and achievement is one of the requisites to further achievement.

—JOHN HOPE FRANKLIN

A man scratches where he can reach.

—ASHANTI PROVERB

*T*o struggle and battle and overcome and absolutely defeat every force designed against us is the only way to achieve.

—NANNIE BURROUGHS

*N*o matter what accomplishments you make, somebody helps you.

—ALTHEA GIBSON

I learned that along with the towering achievements of the cultures of ancient Greece and China there stood the culture of Africa, unseen and denied by the imperialist looters of Africa's material wealth.

—PAUL ROBESON

We now number as many souls as won the freedom of your sires from British rule. We may not *now* be as capable to govern ourselves as they were, but we will, with your aid, be as zealous, and with God's blessing, we will be as successful.

—FROM A PETITION REQUESTING CONGRESS TO RELOCATE FREED SLAVES TO CENTRAL AMERICA, APRIL 1862

I think that art is a celebration of life even when life extends into death and that the sociological conditions which have made for so much misery in Negro life are not necessarily the only factors which make for the values which I feel should endure and shall endure.

—RALPH ELLISON

Africa

O, ye daughters of Africa, awake! arise! no longer sleep nor slumber, but distinguish yourselves. Show forth to the world that ye are endowed with noble and exalted faculties.

—MARIA W. STEWART

I am an African-American, . . . I am not ashamed of my African descent. Africa had great universities before there were any in England and the African was the first man industrious and skillful enough to work in iron. If our group must have a special name setting it apart, the sensible way to settle it would be to refer to our ancestors, the Africans, from whom our swarthy complexions come.

— MARY CHURCH TERRELL

T he African race is a rubber ball; the harder you dash it to the ground, the higher it will rise.

— AFRICAN PROVERB

W e now see that the missionary condescension of past generations in their attitude toward Africa was a pious but sad mistake. In taking it, we have fallen into the snare of enemies and have given grievous offense to our brothers.

— ALAIN LOCKE

. . . *t* he sons and daughters of Africa, will, in spite of all the opposition of their enemies, stand forth in all the dignity and glory that is granted by the Lord to his creature man.

— DAVID WALKER

For I am my mother's daughter, and the drums of Africa still beat in my heart. They will not let me rest while there is a single Negro boy or girl without a chance to prove his worth.

— MARY MCLEOD BETHUNE

Oh, Africa, land of my fathers, my heart bleeds for thy children.

— BLACK CHRONICLE, 1794

When Europe was inhabited by a race of cannibals, a race of savage men, heathens and pagans, Africa was peopled with a race of cultured Black men who were masters in art, science, and literature.

— MARCUS GARVEY

Africa is a Dark Continent not merely because its people are dark-skinned or by reason of its extreme impenetrability, but because its history is lost.

— PAUL ROBESON

What is Africa to me:
Copper sun or scarlet sea,
Jungle star or jungle track,
Strong bronzed men, or regal black
Women from whose loins I sprang
When the birds of Eden sang?
One three centuries removed
From the scenes his father loved,
Spicy grove, cinnamon tree,
What is Africa to me?

— COUNTEE CULLEN

In America, one heard little or nothing about Africa.

— ESLANDA ROBESON

I am of the African race, and in the colour which is natural to them of the deepest dye, and it is under a sense of the most profound gratitude to the Supreme Ruler.

— BENJAMIN BANNEKER

*A*frica is marching forward to freedom, and no power on earth can halt her now.

— KWAME NKRUMAH

*I*t is still yesterday in Africa. It will take millions of tomorrows to rectify what has been done here.

— LORRAINE HANSBERRY

... *m*any powerful sons and daughters of Africa will shortly arise, who will put down vice and immorality among us, and declare ... that they will have their rights; and if refused, I am afraid that they will spread horror and devastation around. I believe that the oppression of injured Africa has come up before the majesty of heaven.

— MARIA W. STEWART

*S*o long,
so far away
Is Africa's
Dark face.

— LANGSTON HUGHES

Age

Ah ain't gittin' ole, honey. Ah'm done ole.

—ZORA NEALE HURSTON

The man who views the world at fifty the same as he did at twenty has wasted thirty years of his life.

—MUHAMMAD ALI

How old would you be if you didn't know how old you are?

—SATCHEL PAIGE

If a man can reach the latter days of his life with his soul intact, he has mastered life.

—GORDON PARKS

*L*ike anybody, I would like to live a long life. Longevity has its place. But I'm not concerned about that now. I just want to do God's will. And He's allowed me to go up to the mountain. And I've looked over. And I have seen the promised land.

—MARTIN LUTHER KING, JR.

*T*he trouble with most women is they get old in their heads. They think about it too much.

—JOSEPHINE BAKER

I am an aged tree, that when I was growing,
uttered a vague sweet sound when the breeze caressed me.
The time for youthful smiles has now passed by;
now, let the hurricane swirl my heart to song!

—RUBEN DARIO

*S*ometimes from the birthstone to the tombstone ain't nothing but a few steps. High ones, low ones. Don't matter. And sometime you don't even know you been walking on the road of time, think you been standin' still and you been flyin' with your feet.

—J. CALIFORNIA COOPER

F or my people lending their strength to the years, to the gone years and the now years and the maybe years, washing ironing cooking scrubbing sewing mending hoeing plowing digging planting pruning patching dragging along never gaining never reaping never knowing and never understanding. . . .

—MARGARET WALKER

Ambition

C an't nothing make your life work if you ain't the architect.

—TERRY McMILLAN

S trive to make something of yourself; then strive to make the most of yourself.

—ALEXANDER CRUMMELL

No matter how far a person can go the horizon is still way beyond you.

— ZORA NEALE HURSTON

Never look behind you, something may be gaining on you.

— SATCHEL PAIGE

If slaves have a bad master, his ambition is to get a better one; when he gets a better, he aspires to have the best; and when he gets the best, he aspires to be his own master.

— FREDERICK DOUGLASS

Aspire to be, and all that we are not God will give us credit for trying.

— NANNIE BURROUGHS

Let a new earth rise. Let another world be born.

— MARGARET WALKER

America

Our minds are made up to live here if we can, or die here if we must; so every attempt to remove us, will be as it ought to be, labor lost. . . . We live here—have lived here—have a right to live here, and mean to live here.

— FREDERICK DOUGLASS

This land which we have watered with our *tears* and our *blood,* is now our *mother country* and we are well satisfied to stay where wisdom abounds and the gospel is free.

— BISHOP RICHARD ALLEN

What a happy country this will be, if the whites will listen.

— DAVID WALKER

*A*merica is me. It gave me the only life I know so I must share in its survival.

— GORDON PARKS

*W*hat is wrong with the United States? We are an intelligent, rich and powerful nation. Yet today we are confused and frightened.

— W. E. B. DU BOIS

*T*he Negro mind reaches out as yet to nothing but American wants, American ideas. But this forced attempt to build his Americanism on race values is a unique social experiment, and its ultimate success is impossible except through the fullest sharing of American culture and institutions.

— ALAIN LOCKE

America needs to understand Islam, because this is the one religion that erases from its society the race problem. Throughout my travels in the Muslim world, I have met, talked to, and even eaten with people who in America would have been considered "white"—but the "white" attitude was removed from their minds by the religion of Islam. I have never before seen *sincere* and *true* brotherhood practiced by all colors together, irrespective of their color.

—MALCOLM X

Our flag is red, white and blue, but our nation is rainbow —red, yellow, brown, black and white—we're all precious in God's sight. America is not like a blanket—one piece of unbroken cloth, the same color, the same texture, the same size. America is more like a quilt—many patches, many pieces, many colors, many sizes, all woven and held together by a common thread.

—JESSE JACKSON

There is nothing so indigenous, so completely "made in America" as we Blacks.

—WILLIAM WELLS-BROWN

We have to undo the millions of little white lies that America told itself and the world about the American Black man.

—JOHN OLIVER KILLENS

The Black man must find himself as a Black man before he can find himself as an American. He must now become a hyphenated American discovering the hyphen so he can eventually lose it.

—JAMES FARMER

America is both racist and anti-feminist.

—SHIRLEY CHISHOLM

We are all simply Americans . . . the unnecessary labeling of people by race . . . or ethnicity does nothing to bring the many diverse groups of American society together.

—BENJAMIN DAVIS, JR.

Whether freeman or slaves the colored race in this country have always looked upon the United States as the Promised Land of Universal freedom, and no earthly temptation has been strong enough to induce us to rebel against it.

—FROM A PETITION TO THE TENNESSEE CONSTITUTIONAL CONVENTION TO GRANT AFRICAN AMERICANS THE RIGHT TO VOTE

. . . the Negro has helped to shape and mold and make America; that he has been a creator as well as a creature; that he has been a giver as well as a receiver. . . . America would not and could not be precisely the America it is, except for the influence, often silent, but nevertheless potent, that the Negro has exercised in its making.

—JAMES WELDON JOHNSON

I love America more than any other country in the world, and, exactly for this reason, I insist on the right to criticize her perpetually.

—JAMES BALDWIN

*T*he position of the Negro in American culture is indeed a paradox. It almost passes understanding how and why a group of people can be socially despised, yet at the same time artistically esteemed and culturally influential, can be both an oppressed minority and a dominant cultural force.

— ALAIN LOCKE

Anger

*F*or it is not light that is needed, but fire; it is not the gentle shower, but thunder. We need the storm, the whirlwind, and the earthquake. The feeling in the nation must be quickened, the conscience of the nation must be roused . . . the hypocrisy of the nation must be exposed; and its crimes against God and man must be denounced.

— FREDERICK DOUGLASS

Your door is shut against my tightened face,
And I am sharp as steel with discontent;
But I possess the courage and the grace
To bear my anger proudly and unbent.

—CLAUDE MCKAY

Angry men seldom fight if their tongues do not lead the fray.

—CHARLES V. ROMAN

You must be willing to suffer the anger of the opponent, and yet not return anger. No matter how emotional your opponents are, you must remain calm.

—MARTIN LUTHER KING, JR.

When you and I develop . . . anger . . . then we'll get some kind of respect and recognition, and some changes from these people who have been promising us falsely already for far too long.

—MALCOLM X

Muffle your rage. Get smart instead of muscular.

— ROY WILKINS

A DREAM DEFERRED

What happens to a dream deferred?
    Does it dry up
    like a raisin in the sun?
    Or fester like a sore—
    And then run?
    Does it stink like rotten meat?
    Or crust and sugar over—
    like a syrupy sweet?

    Maybe it just sags
    like a heavy load.

    Or does it explode?

— LANGSTON HUGHES

Beauty

De mornin'-glories ain't pertickler lubly to man wid de backache.

—FROM A SLAVE NARRATIVE

You are the risen sun, and the early rays of dawn,
Will I ever find your like, you who have been shown to me only once?

—SOMALI POEM, TRANSLATED BY
B. W. ANDRZEJEWSKI AND I. M. LEWIS

My first husband looked like the sun. I used to say his name over and over again till it hung from my ears like diamonds.

—SONIA SANCHEZ

The blacker the berry, the sweeter the juice.

—TRADITIONAL

My blackness, tender and strong, wounded and wise. My blackness is the beauty of the land.

—LANCE JEFFERS

Her skin is like the dusk on the eastern horizon,
O cant you see it, O cant you see it,
Her skin is like dusk on the far eastern horizon
. . . When the sun goes down.

—JEAN TOOMER

You are beautiful; but learn to work, for you cannot eat your beauty.

—CONGOLESE PROVERB

Pretty can only get prettier, but beauty compounds itself.
—EDWARD KENNEDY (''DUKE'') ELLINGTON

The stranger took my beauty and placed it in my hand.
Loveliness beyond the jewels of a throne.

— WOLE SOYINKA

The more blackness a woman has, the more beautiful she is.

— ALEX HALEY

No matter how beautiful the idol, it must rest on a solid base.

— LUBA PROVERB

I had forgot wide fields, and clear brown streams;
The perfect loveliness that God has made,—
Wild violets shy and Heaven-mounting dreams.
And now—unwittingly, you've made me dream
Of violets, and my soul's forgotten gleam.

— ALICE DUNBAR-NELSON

Since Naturally Black is Naturally Beautiful
I must be proud
And, naturally,
Black and
Beautiful
Who always was a trifle
Yellow
And plain though proud
Before.

—AUDRE LORDE

Let a beauty full of healing and strength of final clenching
be the pulsing in our spirits and our blood.

—MARGARET WALKER

I will take from the hearts
of black men—
Prayers their lips
Are 'fraid to utter
And turn their coarseness
Into a beauty of the jungle
Whence they came.

—MAE COWDERY

I have chosen to paint the life of my people as I know and feel it—passionately and dispassionately. It is important that the artist identify with the self-reliance, hope and courage of the people about him, for art must always go where energy is.

—ROMARE BEARDON

I find, in being black, a thing of beauty: a joy; a strength; a secret cup of gladness—a native land in neither time nor place—a native land in every Negro face! Be loyal to yourselves: your skin; your hair; your lips, your southern speech, your laughing kindness—are Negro kingdoms, vast as any other.

—OSSIE DAVIS

Blues

The blues is where we came from and what we experience.
The blues came from nothingness, from want, from desire.

— W. C. HANDY

You see me ravin', you hear me cryin',
Oh Lawd, this lonely heart of mine,
Sometimes, I'm grievin from my hat down to my shoes.
I'm a good hearted woman that's a slave to the blues.

— MA RAINEY

The most astonishing aspect of the blues is that, though replete with a sense of defeat and downheartedness, they are not intrinsically pessimistic; their burden of woe and melancholy is dialectically redeemed through sheer force of sensuality into an exultant affirmation of life, of love, of sex, of movement, of hope.

—RICHARD WRIGHT

The blues slows you down and gives you time to think.

—ALBERT KING

Blues was conceived of by freedmen and ex-slaves as the result of personal or intellectual experiences: an emotional confirmation of, and reaction to, the way in which most Negroes are still forced to exist in the United States.

—LEROI JONES (AMIRI BARAKA)

Blues is joyful. It's a celebration of having overcome bad times.

—JOE WILLIAMS

. . . *p* oor people have the blues because they're poor and hungry. Rich people . . . because they're trying to hold on to their money and everything they have.

— JOHN LEE HOOKER

W hen a woman take the blues, she tuck her head and cry. But when a man catch the blues, he grab his shoes and slide.

— SHERLEY ANNE WILLIAMS

g onna get me a man, who pays for it up front
i say, gonna get me a man, who pays for it up front
cuz when i needs it, can't wait 'til the middle of next month

— SONIA SANCHEZ

W hat did I do
To be so black
And blue?

— LOUIS ARMSTRONG

I wondered why God made me.
I wondered why He made me black.
I wondered why Mama begat me—
And I started to give God His ticket back.

—LERONE BENNETT, JR.

I woke up this morning with the Blues all 'round my bed
Thinking about what you, my baby, said.
Do say the word and give my poor heart ease,
The Blues ain't nothing but a fatal heart disease.

—W. C. HANDY

Brotherhood

*S*ir, we are part and parcel of this nation, which has done more than any other on earth to illustrate the great idea that all races of men may dwell together in harmony. We will take that time-honored flag which has been borne through the heat of a thousand battles. Under its folds Anglo-Saxon and Africo-American can together work out a common destiny, until universal liberty, as announced by this nation, shall be known throughout the world.

—RICHARD CAIN

A sure way for one to lift himself up is by helping to lift someone else.

—BOOKER T. WASHINGTON

I have the people behind me and the people are my strength.

—HUEY P. NEWTON

*W*e must all learn to live together as brothers. Or we will all perish together as fools.

—MARTIN LUTHER KING, JR.

*W*e are inevitably our brother's keeper because we are our brother's brother. Whatever affects one directly affects all indirectly.

—MARTIN LUTHER KING, JR.

A man has to act like a brother before you can call him a brother.

—MALCOLM X

*W*e need to stop idealizing and idolizing the brother on the block. He is no hero. He is a casualty, a victim. And he will remain a pawn, like all of us, until we *live* together, until we all work together to rebuild our family.

—KEORAPETSE KGOSITSILE

I wish I had some way to give the meaning of my life to others . . . to make a bridge from man to man. . . .

—RICHARD WRIGHT

. . . *A*nd I'm gonna put white hands
And black hands and brown and yellow hands
And red clay earth hands in it
Touching everybody with kind fingers
And touching each other natural as dew. . . .

—LANGSTON HUGHES

. . . *n* o man shall cause me to turn my back upon my race. With it I will sink or swim.

—JOHN S. ROCK

L ove yourself and your kind.

—ELIJAH MUHAMMAD

C hallenge

N ow my life is really starting. Fighting injustice, fighting racism, fighting crime, fighting illiteracy, fighting poverty."

—MUHAMMAD ALI

*L*et a new earth rise. Let another world be born. Let a bloody peace be written in the sky. Let a second generation full of courage issue forth; let a people loving freedom come to growth, let a beauty full of healing and a strength of final clenching be the pulsing in our spirits and our bloods. Let the martial songs be written, let the dirges disappear. Let a race of men now rise and take control!

— MARGARET WALKER

*T*he world should not pass judgment upon the Negro, and especially the Negro youth, too quickly or too harshly. The Negro boy has obstacles, discouragements, and temptations to battle with that are little known to those not situated as he is. When a white boy undertakes a task, it is taken for granted that he will succeed. On the other hand, people are usually surprised if the Negro boy does not fail.

— BOOKER T. WASHINGTON

*W*e must use time creatively, and forever realize that the time is always ripe to do right.

— MARTIN LUTHER KING, JR.

Oh, deep in my heart,
I do believe, that
We shall overcome
Someday.

—CIVIL RIGHTS SONG

May we rise to the challenge to struggle for our rights. Come what will or may and let us never falter.

—A. PHILIP RANDOLPH

The challenge is in the moment, the time is always now.

—JAMES BALDWIN

... the challenge facing us is to equip ourselves that we will be able to take our place wherever we are in the affairs of men.

—BARBARA JORDAN

We are challenged to see that the barriers of yesterday . . . are not replaced by new barriers of apathy, of underdeveloped skills, of lack of training.

—WHITNEY YOUNG, JR.

My challenge to the young people is to pick up where this generation has left off, to create a world where every man, woman, and child is not limited, except by their own capabilities.

—COLIN POWELL

A large ship may still be wrecked in darkness.

—AFRICAN PROVERB

The Black University already exists; it's for us to recognize it, not create it. And this is good. Our work is crystal-clear. The question is, are we teachers ready to learn—are we leaders ready to follow?

—NIKKI GIOVANNI

... *W*hat would it be like if black people ruled the earth ... ? Surely, no worse than what white men had put us through and maybe, given what we knew, a good deal better.

— SHERLEY ANNE WILLIAMS

*I*f we—and I mean the relatively conscious whites and the relatively conscious blacks, who must, like lovers, insist on, or create the consciousness of others—do not falter in our duty now, we may be able, handful that we are, to end the racial nightmare of our country and change the history of the world.

— JAMES BALDWIN

*I*n the next phase of Afro-American writing, a literature of celebration must be created—not a celebration of oppression, but a celebration of survival in spite of it.

— JOHN HENRIK CLARKE

... *O*ne must find ... one's own moral center and move through the world hoping that this center will guide one aright.

— JAMES BALDWIN

We learn the rope of life by untying its knots.

—JEAN TOOMER

Confidence

I was going to beat Schmeling. The mind is a powerful thing. From the tip of my toes to the last hair on my head, I had complete confidence.

—JOE LOUIS

I have confidence not only in my country and her institutions but in the endurance, capacity and destiny of my people.

—BLANCHE K. BRUCE

I've always had confidence. It came because I have lots of initiative. I wanted to make something of myself.

—EDDIE MURPHY

*I*f you don't have confidence, you'll always find a way not to win.

—CARL LEWIS

*O*nce I get the ball you're at my mercy. There's nothing you can say or do about it. I own the ball, I own the game, I own the guy guarding me.

—MICHAEL JORDAN

*W*hen the mouse laughs at the cat, there is a hole nearby.

—BENIN PROVERB

Courage

West Point, June 29, 1870

*D*ear Friend:
Your kind letter should have been answered long ere this, but really I have been so harassed that I could not do anything. I

passed the examination all right but my companion Howard was rejected. Since he went away I have been lonely indeed. These fellows appear to be trying their utmost to run me off, and I fear they will succeed. We went into camp yesterday and all night they were around my tent cursing and swearing at me so that I did not sleep two hours. It is just the same at the table, and what I get to eat I must snatch for it like a dog.

The one who drills the squad is the meanest specimen of humanity I ever saw. This morning he said to me, "Stand off from the line, you damned black—. I want you to remember you are not on an equal footing with the white men and what you learn you will have to pick up, for I won't teach you a damned thing."

I have borne insult upon insult until I am completely worn out. I wish I had some good news for you, but alas! it seems to be getting worse and worse. I hope my brightest hopes will be realized, but I doubt if they will ever be here.

JAMES W. SMITH
[THE FIRST BLACK ADMITTED TO WEST POINT]
New Era, July 14, 1870

Columbia, South Carolina, July 3, 1870

M y Dear Son:
I pray God my letter may find you in a better state than when you wrote me. I told you that you would have trials to endure. Do not mind them, for they will go like the chaff

before the wind and your enemies will soon be glad to gain your friendship. They do the same to newcomers in every college. Do not let them run you away, for then they will say the "nigger" won't do. Show your spunk and let them see that you will fight. That is what you are sent to West Point for.

You must not resign on any account for that is what the Democrats want. They are betting here that they will devil you so much that you can't stay. Stand your ground, don't resign and write me soon.

From your affectionate father, ISRAEL SMITH [A FORMER SLAVE]

New Era, July 21, 1870

I now resolved that, however long I might remain a slave in form, the day had passed forever when I could be a slave in fact. I did not hesitate to let it be known of me, that the white man who expected to succeed in whipping me, must also succeed in killing me.

—FREDERICK DOUGLASS

I would fight for my liberty so long as my strength lasted, and if the time came for me to go, the Lord would let them take me.

—HARRIET TUBMAN

I am a good American, the colored people are good people. The valor of the colored people was tested on many battlefields and today their bones lie bleaching beside every hill and every valley from the Potomac to the Gulf.

—JAMES RAPIER

L ose not courage, lose not faith, go forward.

—MARCUS GARVEY

C ourage is one step ahead of fear.

—COLEMAN YOUNG

O ne isn't necessarily born with courage, but one is born with potential. Without courage, we cannot practice any other virtue with consistency. We can't be kind, true, merciful, generous, or honest.

—MAYA ANGELOU

These are the days for strong men to courageously expose wrong.

—ADAM CLAYTON POWELL, JR.

You stand on the border-line wondering what's beyond. Then you take one step and you feel a strange, sweet tingling. You take two steps and the feeling becomes keener. You want to feel some more. You break into a run. You know it's dangerous, but you're propelled in spite of yourself.

—NEW MASSES, OCTOBER 8, 1935

. . . the courage to live life, in and from its belly as well as beyond its edges, to see and say what it was to recognize and identify evil, but never fear or stand in awe of it.

—TONI MORRISON

Any man's a coward who won't die for what he believes.

—CHESTER B. HIMES

Culture

O ur folk culture is like the growth of some hardy yet exotic shrub whose fragrance never fails to delight the discriminating nostrils even when there is no interest in the depth of its roots. But when the leaves are gathered by strange hands they soon wither and when cuttings are transplanted into strange soil they have but a short and sickly life. Only those who sowed may know the secret of the root.

— HALL JOHNSON

To Break Up a Love Affair

Take nine needles, break each needle in three pieces. Write each person's name three times on paper. Write one name backwards and one forwards and lay the broken needles on the paper. Take five black candles, four red and three green.

Tie a string across the door from it, suspend a large candle upside down. It will hang low on the door; burn one each day for one hour. If you burn your first in the daytime, keep on in the day; if at night, continue at night. A tin plate with paper and needles in it must be placed to catch wax in.

When the ninth day is finished, go out into the street and get some white or black dog dung. A dog only drops his dung in the tree when he is running and barking, and whoever you curse will run and bark likewise. Put it in a bag with the paper and carry it to running water, and one of the parties will leave town.

— ZORA NEALE HURSTON

The road for the serious black artist, then, who would produce a racial art is most certainly rocky and the mountain is high.

— LANGSTON HUGHES

It was like homecoming, and I felt I had penetrated to the core of African culture when I began to study the legendary traditions, folk-song and folklore of the West African.

— PAUL ROBESON

... *t* he most apparent legacies of the African past, even to the contemporary Black American ... blues, jazz, and the adaptation of the Christian religion, all rely heavily on African culture.

—LEROI JONES (AMIRI BARAKA)

D estroy the culture and you destroy the people.

—FRANTZ FANON

Y ou do not inherit culture and artistic skill through your genes. These come as a result of personal conquest, of the individual's applying himself to that art, that music ... which helps him to realize and complete himself.

—RALPH ELLISON

M y approach to solving social problems is through the arts, the arts give you a discipline and a structure.

—ARTHUR MITCHELL

This is the only real concern of the artist, to re-create out of the disorder of life that order which is art.

—JAMES BALDWIN

Brilliant wit will shine from whence it will.

—MARIA W. STEWART

. . . I haven't found the problem of being a Negro in any sense a hindrance to putting words on paper. It may be a hindrance sometimes to selling them.

—LANGSTON HUGHES

There is no need to establish a "black aesthetic." Rather, it is important to understand that one already exists.

—LAURENCE P. NEAL

To explore the black experience means that we do not deny the reality and the power of the slave culture; the culture that produced the blues, spirituals, folk songs, work songs, and "jazz." It means that Afro-American life and its myriad of styles are expressed and examined in the fullest, most truthful manner possible.

—LAURENCE P. NEAL

feverish ecstasy was followed by that contentment—that sense of serene joy—which makes artistic creation the most complete of all human experiences.

—JAMES WELDON JOHNSON

Great art can only be created out of love.

—JAMES BALDWIN

Death

I WANT TO DIE WHILE YOU LOVE ME

I want to die while you love me,
While yet you hold me fair,
While laughter lies upon my lips
And lights are in my hair.

I want to die while you love me,
I could not bear to see,
The glory of this perfect day,
Grow dim—or cease to be.

I want to die while you love me,
Oh! Who would care to live
Till love has nothing more to ask
And nothing more to give.

I want to die while you love me
And never, never see
The glory of this perfect day
Grow dim or cease to be.

— GEORGIA DOUGLAS JOHNSON

I am not going to die, I'm going home like a shooting star.

— SOJOURNER TRUTH

B ecause I had loved so deeply,
Because I had loved so long,
God in His great compassion
Gave me the gift of song.
Because I had loved so vainly,
And sung with such faltering breath,
The Master in infinite mercy
Offers the boon of Death.

— PAUL LAURENCE DUNBAR

I f you're afraid to die, you will not be able to live.

— JAMES BALDWIN

Many dogs are the death of the lion.

—SOMALI PROVERB

i cry
the morning song
go away death
go from love's house
go make your empty bed

—BELL HOOKS

When brothers fight to death a stranger inherits their father's estate.

—IBO PROVERB

We have slumbered and slept too long already; the day is far spent; the night of death approaches.

—MARIA W. STEWART

DEATH—A FUNERAL SUMMONS

And Death heard the summons,
And he leaped on his fastest horse,
Pale as a sheet in the moonlight.
Up the golden street Death galloped.

—JAMES WELDON JOHNSON

The first dying to be done by the black man will be done to make himself free.

—MARCUS GARVEY

He had seen death coming and had stood his ground and fought it . . . to the last breath. Naturally he didn't have time to straighten himself out. Death had to take him like it found him.

—ZORA NEALE HURSTON

Man dies when he refuses to stand up for that which is right. A man dies when he refuses to take a stand for that which is true.

—MARTIN LUTHER KING, JR.

*E*ach man's death is fated from the beginning of time.

—FRANK YERBY

*D*eath mattered not—It was a mere punctuation.

—NATHAN HUGGINS

*D*eath cannot put the brakes on a good dream.

—MARVA COLLINS

*I*f you're going to die, die doing what you love to do.

—BERNARD SHAW

*I*t has always been my belief that I, too, will die by violence. I have done all that I can to be prepared.

—MALCOLM X

. . . *s*eeing the world through white eyes from a black soul causes death.

—CLARENCE MAJOR

Despair

I am tired of work; I am tired of building up somebody else's civilization. . . . Throw the children into the river; civilization has given us too many. It is better to die than it is to grow up and find out that you are colored. Pluck the stars out of the heavens. The stars mark our destiny. I am tired of civilization.

—FENTON JOHNSON

*N*o people need ever despair whose women are fully aroused to the duties which rest upon them and are willing to shoulder responsibilities which they alone can successfully assume.

—MARY CHURCH TERRELL

Only a man who has felt ultimate despair is capable of feeling ultimate bliss.

—ALEXANDRE DUMAS

Despair? Did someone say despair was a question in the world? Well, then, listen to the sons of those who have known little else if you wish to know the resiliency of this thing you would so quickly resign to mythhood, this thing called the human spirit.

—LORRAINE HANSBERRY

There comes a time when the cup of endurance runs over, and men are no longer willing to be plunged into an abyss of injustice, where they experience the blackness of corroding despair.

—MARTIN LUTHER KING, JR.

Difficulty need not foreshadow despair or defeat. Rather achievement can be all the more satisfying because of obstacles surmounted.

—WILLIAM HASTIE

S orrow is like rice in the store; if a basketful is removed every day, it will come to an end at last.

— SOMALI PROVERB

f or my people walking blindly spreading joy, losing time being lazy, sleeping when hungry, shouting when burdened, drinking when hopeless, tied and shackled and tangled among ourselves by the unseen creatures who tower over us omnisciently and laugh. . . .

— MARGARET WALKER

Dignity

I will not take *but* for an answer.

— LANGSTON HUGHES

*M*ake a law that will meet the demands of justice without maiming the body, crippling the intellect, brutalizing the man.

—GEORGE TEAMOH

I am somebody.

—JESSE JACKSON

*D*o a common thing in an uncommon way.

—BOOKER T. WASHINGTON

*Y*ou cannot live with a chip on your shoulder even if you can manage a smile around your eyes— For chips make you bend your body to balance them. And once you bend, you lose your poise, your balance, and the chip gets into you. The real you. You get hard.

—MARITA BONNER

Man, in all ages and all nations of the earth, is the same. Man is a peculiar creature—he is the image of God, though he may be subjected to the most wretched condition upon earth, yet the spirit and feeling which constitute the creature, man, can never be entirely erased from his breast, because God who made him after his own image, planted it in his heart; he cannot get rid of it.

—DAVID WALKER

To be dependent is to be degraded.

—AN ADDRESS TO THE COLORED PEOPLE OF THE UNITED STATES FROM THE COLORED NATIONAL CONVENTION OF 1848

No race can prosper till it learns that there is as much dignity in tilling a field as in writing a poem.

—BOOKER T. WASHINGTON

When the battle is won, let history be able to say to each one of us: He was a dedicated patriot. Dignity was his country, Manhood was his government and Freedom was his land.

—JOHN OLIVER KILLENS

*H*uman dignity is more precious than prestige.

— CLAUDE MCKAY

*L*ife should be lived with dignity, the personalities of others shouldn't be violated, that men should be able to confront other men without fear or shame, and that if men were lucky in their living on earth, they might win some redeeming meaning for their having struggled and suffered here beneath the stars.

— RICHARD WRIGHT

*N*ow is the time to make real the promise of democracy, and transform our pending national elegy into a creative psalm of brotherhood. Now is the time to lift our national policy from the quicksand of racial injustice to the solid rock of human dignity.

— MARTIN LUTHER KING, JR.

*Y*ou will see that from the start we tried to dignify our race. If I am to be condemned for that I am satisfied.

— MARCUS GARVEY

*M*ankind through the ages has been in a ceaseless struggle to give dignity and meaning to human life. It is that quest which separates it from the animal.

—MARTIN LUTHER KING, JR.

*T*here is no dignity without freedom.

—SÉKOU TOURÉ

... *p*rotest literature is finally a plea to white America for our human dignity. We cannot get it that way. We must address each other. We must touch each other's beauty, wonder, and pain.

—LAURENCE P. NEAL

*T*he trick is to accept what makes you good.

—JAMES BALDWIN

I will not feed your hunger with my blood
Nor crown your nakedness
With jewels of my elegant pain.

—NAOMI LONG MADGETT

. . . the Negro experience has bred something mystical and strangely different in the Negro soul.

—ALAIN LOCKE

Discrimination

When I played against white players in the early days, the linesmen didn't always call them out. I learned that there was no use complaining, but I also learned that I could win anyway.

—ARTHUR ASHE

*U*ntil the killing of black men, black mothers' sons, becomes as important as the killing of white men, white mothers' sons, we who believe in freedom cannot rest.

— ELLA J. BAKER

I was thinking about all the honors that are showered on me in the theater, how everyone wishes to shake my hand or get an autograph, a real hero you'd naturally think. However, when I reach a hotel, I am refused permission to ride on the passenger elevator, I cannot enter the dining room for my meals, and am Jim Crowed generally. . . . I know this to be an unbelievable custom.

— BERT WILLIAMS

*W*e have pursued the shadow, they have obtained the substance; we have performed the labor, they have received the profits; we have planted the vines, they have eaten the fruits of them.

— MARIA W. STEWART

White men began printing long before Colored men dared read their works; had power to establish any rule they saw fit. As a mark of disrespect, as a stigma, as a badge of inferiority, they tacitly agreed to spell his name without a capital.

— IDA B. WELLS

As with the Jew, persecution is making the Negro international.

— ALAIN LOCKE

Hate demands existence, and he who hates has to show his hate in appropriate actions and behaviors; in a sense, he has to become hate. That is why the Americans have substituted discrimination for lynching.

— FRANTZ FANON

. . . the competence and attainments of the attorneys we often dealt with were no higher than ours, but their superior position was maintained and protected by white skins.

— NELSON MANDELA

Discrimination and intolerance will eat you up and destroy whatever creativity was in you if you let it.

— GORDON PARKS

The black man in North American was spiritually sick because for centuries he had accepted the white man's Christianity—which asked the black so-called Christian to expect no true Brotherhood of man but to endure the cruelties of the white so-called Christians.

— MALCOLM X

I didn't know there were so many ways of saying "no" without ever once using the word. . . . Sometimes I'd find myself in the elevator, on my way out, and smiling all over myself because I thought I had gotten the job, before it would hit me that they had really said no, not yes.

— PAULE MARSHALL

I could not accept the ghetto, and ironclad residential restrictions against Negroes situated as we were made escape impossible, confining us to neighborhoods where we had to fly home each evening before darkness fell and honest people abandoned the streets to predators.

— ARNA BONTEMPS

*A*fter the Egyptian and Indian, the Greek and Roman, the Teuton and Mongolian, the Negro is a sort of seventh son, born with a veil, and gifted with second-sight in this American world—a world which yields him no true self-consciousness, but only lets him see himself through the revelation of the other world.

— W. E. B. DU BOIS

. . . *t*he color of the skin is in no ways connected with strength of the mind or intellectual powers. . . .

— BENJAMIN BANNEKER

Dreams

And now—unwittingly, you've made me dream
Of violets, and my soul's forgotten gleam.

—ALICE DUNBAR-NELSON

DREAMS
Hold fast to dreams
For if dreams die
Life is a broken-winged bird
That cannot fly.
Hold fast to dreams
For when dreams go
Life is a barren field
Frozen with snow.

—LANGSTON HUGHES

We need visions for larger things, for the unfolding and reviewing of worthwhile things.

—MARY MCLEOD BETHUNE

It isn't a calamity to die with dreams unfulfilled, but it is a calamity not to dream.

—BENJAMIN E. MAYS

We stand in life at midnight; we are always on the threshold of a new dawn.

—MARTIN LUTHER KING, JR.

Dreams [can be] mocked to death by Time.

—ZORA NEALE HURSTON

Is this real, this fascination? Are my dreams holding you fast?

—FATS WALLER

[A] dream [is] the bearer of a new possibility, the enlarged horizon, the great hope.

—HOWARD THURMAN

SLEEP
The soft grey hands of sleep
Toiled all night long
To spin a beautiful garment
Of dreams.

—EDWARD SILVERA

Sometimes my dreams are so deep that I dream that I'm dreaming.

—RAY CHARLES

The dream is real, my friends. The failure to make it work is the unreality.

—TONI CADE BAMBARA

We don't have an eternity to realize our dreams, only the time we are are here.

— SUSAN KING TAYLOR

The dreams have been cashed in for reality and reality is so much sweeter than the dream.

— PHILIP MICHAEL THOMAS

The only thing that will stop you from fulfilling your dreams is you.

— TOM BRADLEY

[W] hat do you pack when you pursue a dream? And what do you leave behind?

— SANDRA SHARP

Shadow

Shadow.
I am black.
I lie down in the shadow.
No longer the light of my dream before me,
Above me.
Only the thick wall.
Only the shadow.
My hands!
My dark hands!
Break through the wall!
Find my dream!
Help me to shatter this darkness,
To smash this night,
To break this shadow
Into a thousand lights of sun,
Into a thousand whirling dreams
Of sun!

—Langston Hughes

. . . I fashioned the wrong dreams.
I wanted to dress like Juliet and act
Before applauding audiences on Broadway.
I learned more about Shakespeare than he knew about
   himself.

But of course, all that was impossible.
"Talent, yes," they would tell me,
"But an actress has to look the part."
So I ended up waiting on tables in Harlem
And hearing uncouth men yell at me:
"Hey, momma, you can cancel that hamburger
And come on up to 102."

— NAOMI LONG MADGETT

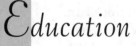

Education

F ree workmen in the cotton field
And in the sugar cane;
Free children in the common school
With nevermore a chain.

— BLACK REPUBLICAN, April 29, 1865

T he record of the teachers of the first colored schools in
Louisiana will be one of honor and blood.

— NEW ORLEANS TRIBUNE, September 5, 1866

To remove prejudices the most natural method would be to allow children five or six years of age to mingle in schools together. Under such training, prejudice must eventually die out; but if we postpone it until they become men and women, prejudice will be so established that no mortal can obliterate it.

—FRANCIS L. CARDOZO

I wants my children to be educated because I can believe what they tells me. If I go to another person with a letter in my hand, he can tell me what he pleases in that letter and I don't know any better. But if I have got children who read and write, they will tell me the contents of that letter and I will know it's all right.

—A LOUISIANA FREEDMAN

And yet politics, and surely American politics, is hardly a school for great minds.

—ANNA J. COOPER

Education comes in drips and drops to a feller who never went to school.

—ROSA GUY

There is no defense or security for any of us except in the highest intelligence and development of all.

—BOOKER T. WASHINGTON

We must do something and we must do it now. We must educate the white people out of their two hundred fifty years of slave history.

—IDA B. WELLS

The Negro race, like all races, is going to be saved by its exceptional men. . . . Men we shall have only as we make manhood the object of the work of the schools—intelligence, broad sympathy, knowledge of the world that was and is, and of the relation of men to it—this is the curriculum of that Higher Education which must underlie true life.

—W. E. B. DU BOIS

A system of education is not one thing, nor does it have a single definite object, nor is it a mere matter of schools. Education is that whole system of human training within and without the school house walls, which molds and develops men.

—W. E. B. DU BOIS

Raise the mothers above the level of degradation, and the offspring is elevated with them.

—MARTIN DELANY

There was never a time in my youth, no matter how dark and discouraging the days might be, when one resolve did not continually remain with me, and that was a determination to secure an education at any cost.

—BOOKER T. WASHINGTON

Education is the jewel casting brilliance into the future.

—MARI EVANS

Education is all a matter of building bridges.

—RALPH ELLISON

Education in the past has been too much inspiration and too little information.

—E. FRANKLIN FRAZIER

*P*rejudice is not so much dependent upon natural antipathy as upon education.

—DAVID RUGGLES

*T*o make me believe that those men who have regulated education in our country have humanity in their hearts, is to make me believe a lie.

—ROBERT PURVIS

*O*ne's work may be finished someday, but one's education never.

—ALEXANDRE DUMAS

*E*ducation was feared by slave owners because slaves might read of their national rights.

—BLACK CHRONICLE, JUNE 1, 1896

*E*ducation must not simply teach work—it must teach life.

—W. E. B. DU BOIS

*E*ducation is the key to unlock the golden door of freedom.
— GEORGE WASHINGTON CARVER

*T*o see your enemy and know him is part of the complete education of man. . . .

— MARCUS GARVEY

*T*he function of education is to teach one to think intensively and to think critically. Intelligence plus character— that is the goal of true education.

— MARTIN LUTHER KING, JR.

*I*ntegration and education are not synonymous.

— JAMES BALDWIN

*Y*ou can't legislate good will—that comes through education.

— MALCOLM X

All education is self-acquired, since no one can educate another.

— CHARLES G. ADAMS

If you understand the beginning well, the end will not trouble you.

— ASHANTI PROVERB

What deserts might be reborn, what cities built, what children saved with one third wasted to build bombs we can't afford to use.

— JAMES BALDWIN

We must educate the heart—Teach it hatred of oppression, Truest love of God and man . . .

— CHARLOTTE FORTEN [GRIMKÉ]

IT'S BOUND TO BE BETTER—IF IT'S BLACK. That should be the first lesson taught at any Black institute.

— NIKKI GIOVANNI

H istory is not a procession of illustrious people. It's about what happens to a people. Millions of anonymous people is what history is about.

—JAMES BALDWIN

E ducation meant the death of the institution of slavery in this country, and the slave owners took good care that their slaves got none of it.

—NAT LOVE

I t is impossible to raise and educate a race in the mass. All revolutions and improvements must start with individuals.

—JOHN WESLEY EDWARD BOWEN

Effort

*E*very creature has got an instinct—the calf goes to the cow to suck, the bee to the hive. We's a poor humble degraded people but we know our friends. We'd walk fifteen miles in wartime to find out about the battle. We can walk fifteen miles and more to find out how to vote.

— LOYAL GEORGIAN, April 10, 1867

*T*he gentleman talks about the colored people deteriorating. Sir, who tills your lands now? Who plants your corn? Who raises your cotton? I have traveled over the Southern States and have seen who did this work. Going along, I saw the white men do the smoking, chewing tobacco, riding horses, playing cards, spending money; while the colored men are tilling the soil and bringing the cotton, rice and other products to market.

— RICHARD CAIN

We form a spoke in the human wheel and it is necessary that we should understand out dependence on the different parts, and theirs on us, in order to perform our part with propriety.

— EDITORIAL FROM THE FIRST EDITION OF
FREEDOM'S JOURNAL

Service is the rent you pay for room on this earth.

— SHIRLEY CHISHOLM

The wind of the race's destiny stirs more briskly because of her striving.

— ELISE JOHNSON McDOUGALD

You gotta sing . . .
You gotta moan . . .
You gotta picket . . .
You gotta vote . . .
You gotta move . . .
You gotta pray . . .
You gotta preach . . .
You gotta shout . . .
You gotta rock . . .

You gotta cool it . . .
You gotta love . . .
You gotta die . . .
 —SELMA, ALABAMA, VOTER-REGISTRATION-DRIVE
SONG, 1964

 he wrongs of our brethren, should be our constant theme. There should be no time too precious, no calling too holy, no place too sacred, to make room for this cause. We should not only feel it to be the cause of humanity, but the cause of christianity [*sic*], and fit work for men and angels.
 —AN ADDRESS TO THE COLORED PEOPLE OF THE
UNITED STATES FROM THE COLORED NATIONAL
CONVENTION OF 1848

 alk, without effort, is nothing.
 —MARIA W. STEWART

 he majority of people in the world don't do what it takes to win. Everyone is looking for the easy road.
 —CHARLES BARKLEY

I hope never to be at peace. I hope to make my life manageable, and I think it's fairly manageable now. But, oh, I would never accept peace. That means death.

— JAMAICA KINCAID

I had to make my own living and my own opportunity. . . . Don't sit down and wait for the opportunities to come; you have to get up and make them.

— MADAME C. J. WALKER

[T] he battles that count aren't the ones for gold medals. The struggles within yourself—the invisible, inevitable battles inside all of us—that's where it's at.

— JESSE OWENS

I t is the "man farthest down" who is most active in getting up.

— ALAIN LOCKE

We're gonna ride for civil rights
We're gonna ride both black and white.
Keep your eyes on the prize,
Hold on, hold on.

— CIVIL RIGHTS SONG

Let us not try to be the best or worst of others, but let us make the effort to be the best of ourselves.

— MARCUS GARVEY

Every try will not succeed. If you live, your business is trying.

— JOHN OLIVER KILLENS

We will water the thorn for the sake of the rose.

— KANEM PROVERB

*A*lways being in a hurry does not prevent death, neither does going slowly prevent living.

— IBO PROVERB

*E*very man who lives under the Government should feel that it is his property, his treasure, the bulwark and defence of himself and his family, his pearl of great price, which he must preserve, protect, and defend faithfully at all times, on all occasions, in every possible manner.

— FROM A PETITION TO THE TENNESSEE
CONSTITUTIONAL CONVENTION TO GRANT
AFRICAN AMERICANS THE RIGHT TO VOTE

*I*t is of no use for us to sit with our hands folded, hanging our heads like bulrushes, lamenting our wretched condition; but let us make a mighty effort, and arise; and if no one will promote or respect us, let us promote and respect ourselves.

— MARIA W. STEWART

*W*e will change society or it will be changed for us.

— JAMES BALDWIN

Equality

The white man is always trying to nose into somebody else's business. All right, I'll set something outside the door of my mind for him to play with and handle. He can read my writing but he sho' can't read my mind. Then I'll say my say and sing my song.

— ZORA NEALE HURSTON

We ask for no special privileges or favors. We ask only for even-handed Justice. We simply ask that we shall be recognized as men.

— PROCEEDINGS OF THE COLORED PEOPLE'S
CONVENTION OF THE STATE OF SOUTH CAROLINA
(CHARLESTON, 1865)

We want every man to vote, hold office, sit on juries, travel on steamboats, eat in any restaurant, drink in any saloon, dine at any hotel, or educate our children at any school we choose. We demand equal privileges with the whites in all things. We must elect as many of our own race as we can, join with our Southern loyalists, choose good men from among them. But be sure to vote for no rebel or secessionist, for if you do, you are pulling the hemp to hang yourself with.

—DR. R. I. CROMWELL, NEW ORLEANS TRIBUNE,
APRIL 25, 1867

Look. I stretch out my arms. See; I have two of them, as you have. Look at our ears; I have two of them. I have two eyes, two nostrils, one mouth, two feet. I stand erect like you. I am clothed with humanity like you. I think, I reason, I talk, I express my views as you do. Is there any difference between us?

—RICHARD CAIN

I have been forty years a slave and forty years free, and would be here forty years more to have equal rights for all.

—SOJOURNER TRUTH

We have built up your country. We have worked in your fields, and garnered your harvests, for two hundred and fifty years! Do we ask you for compensation for the tears you have caused, and the hearts you have broken, and the lives you have curtailed and the blood you have spilled? We are willing to let the dead past bury its dead; but we ask you, now, for our RIGHTS.

—HENRY McNEAL TURNER

God is just; when he created man he made him in his image, and never intended one should misuse the other. All men are born free and equal in his sight.

—SUSAN KING TAYLOR

... while you keep us and our children in bondage, and treat us like brutes, to make us support you, and your families, we cannot be your friends.

—DAVID WALKER

*N*ever refuse to act with a white society or institution because it is white, or a black one, because it is black; but act with all men without distinction of color.

—AN ADDRESS TO THE COLORED PEOPLE OF THE
UNITED STATES FROM THE COLORED NATIONAL
CONVENTION OF 1848

*W*ith few exceptions, the Negro youth must work harder and must perform his tasks even better than a white youth in order to secure recognition. But out of the hard and unusual struggle through which he is compelled to pass, he gets a strength, a confidence, that one misses whose pathway is comparatively smooth by reason of birth and race.

—BOOKER T. WASHINGTON

*T*o be free—to walk the good American earth as equal citizens, to live without fear, to enjoy the fruits of our toil, to give our children every opportunity in life—that dream which we have held so long in our hearts is today the destiny that we hold in our hands.

—PAUL ROBESON

The fiction is that the life of the races is separate, and increasingly so. The fact is that they have touched too closely at the unfavorable and too lightly at the favorable levels.

—ALAIN LOCKE

The American Negro demands equality—political equality, industrial equality and social equality; and he is never going to rest satisfied with anything less.

—W. E. B. DU BOIS

The only way to get equality is for two people to get the same thing at the same time at the same place.

—THURGOOD MARSHALL

Equality is the heart and essence of democracy, freedom, and justice.

—A. PHILIP RANDOLPH

Equality cannot be seized any more than it can be given. It must be a shared experience.

— JAMES FARMER

There are two places on earth where human equality is absolute: in the grave and in a prison cell.

— FRANK YERBY

You learn about equality in history and civics, but you find out life is not really like that.

— ARTHUR ASHE

The rain does not recognize anyone as a friend; it drenches all equally.

— IBO PROVERB

He who treats you as himself does you no injustice.

— LON PROVERB

*I*f we are to Receive as much as White Soldiers or the Regular thirteen Dollars per Month then we Shall be Satisfied and on the field of Battle we will prove that we were worthy of what we claim for our Rights.

— WM. J. BROWN, A FREEBORN
AFRICAN-AMERICAN UNION SERGEANT

... *w*hy should one worm say to another, "Keep you down there, while I sit up yonder; for I am better than thou?" It is not the color of the skin that makes the man, but the principles formed within the soul.

— MARIA W. STEWART

*A*s an American Negro, I consider the most fortunate thing in my whole life to be the fact that through childhood I was reared free from undue fear of or esteem for white people as a race; otherwise, the deeper implications of American race prejudice might have become a part of my subconscious as well as of my conscious self.

— JAMES WELDON JOHNSON

We do not ask for the privilege of citizenship, wishing to shun the obligations imposed by it.

— FROM A PETITION TO THE TENNESSEE
CONSTITUTIONAL CONVENTION TO GRANT
AFRICAN AMERICANS THE RIGHT TO VOTE

I just want to know how come Adam and Eve was white. If they had started out black, this world might not be in the fix it is today. Eve might not of paid that serpent no attention. I never did know a Negro yet that liked a snake.

— LANGSTON HUGHES

To be born in a free society and not be born free is to be born into a lie.

— JAMES BALDWIN

It is quite possible to say that the price a Negro pays for becoming articulate is to find himself, at length, with nothing to be articulate about.

— JAMES BALDWIN

. . . *f* or generations in the mind of America, the Negro has been more of a formula than a human being—a something to be argued about, condemned or defended, to be "kept down," or "in his place," or "helped up," to be worried with or worried over, harassed or patronized, a social bogey or a social burden.

—ALAIN LOCKE

. . . *g* ood art transcends land, race, or nationality, and color drops away.

—LANGSTON HUGHES

I n Dixie there are two worlds, the white world and the black world, and they are physically separated. There are white schools and black schools, white churches and black churches, white businesses and black businesses, white grave-yards and black graveyards, and, for all I know, a white God and a black God.

—RICHARD WRIGHT

W e wish to plead our own cause. Too long have others spoken for us.

—JOHN BROWNE RUSSWURM

In being, I am equal.

—JEAN TOOMER

Nature created no races.

—JOHN HENRIK CLARKE

fear

The fact is that the flood of light that has ruled the minds of men since the late war concerning the mental, moral and physical possibilities of the Negro as the coming man of a higher and better civilization, strikes terror to the hearts of men who have so long trampled him underfoot.

—JONATHAN C. GIBBS

So many cares to vex the day,
So many fears to haunt the night . . .

—LESLIE PINCKNEY HILL

Working class boys, we asks you to save us from being burnt on the electric chair. We's only poor working class boys whose skin is black. We shouldn't die for that.
— EIGHT OF THE ''SCOTTSBORO BOYS,'' NEGRO WORKER, MAY 1932

Fear is a noose that binds until it strangles.
— JEAN TOOMER

We have allowed cowardice and fear to take possession of us for a long time, but that will never take us anywhere.
— MARCUS GARVEY

I am one of those troubled hearts,
Fearing the night, fearing the day.
— RENÉ MARAN

There can be no courage without fear, and fear comes only from the imagination.
— PETER ABRAHAMS

*f*ear brings out the worst thing in everybody.

—MAYA ANGELOU

*f*ear and terror scrape out the bottom of one's soul.

—ANTHONY SLOANE

*H*e who has been stung by a serpent fears a rope on the ground.

—SOMALI PROVERB

*U*ntil my mid-teens I lived in fear; fear of being shot, lynched or beaten to death—not for any wrong doing of my own. I could easily have been the victim of mistaken identity or an act of terror by hate-filled white men.

—GORDON PARKS

$f$olklore

I 'm going to put gris-gris
All over their front steps
And make them shake
Until they stutter!

—MARIE LAVEAU

New Jerusalem

De talles' tree in Paradise
De Christian calls de Tree ob Life,
An' I hope dat trumpet blow me home
To my New Jerusalem.

Blow Gabriel! Trumpet, blow louder, louder!
An I hope dat trumpet blow me home
To my New Jerusalem!

Paul and Silas jail-bound
Sing God's praise both night and day,
An' I hope dat trumpet blow me home
To my New Jerusalem!

— GULLAH ANTHEM

W hen folkses on our plantation died, Marster always let many of us as wanted to go lay off work 'til after the burying. Sometimes it were two or three months after the burying before the funeral sermon was preached.

— JAMES BOLTON, A FORMER SLAVE

riest or Priestess: Blood is again melting and falling like rain.

All: Indeed the life-breath, blood is again melting and falling like rain
Blood going like rain; blood going like rain.
Blood, blood, going like rain, blood.

— SACRIFICIAL RITE TO WARRIOR DEITY

*I*f you want to be a evil fortune teller, take and kill a black cat, and take the bones out of the top of the cat's head, and a teaspoon of brains, and a bone out of the cat's neck, and a chicken wishbone; then go out to the four corners of the road on a very dark night—if it is raining that would make it still better—holding all these things in your left hand. Then turn your back first on the east, swearing, using the Lord's Name in vain; then turn back on the north, swearing, using the Lord's Name in vain; then the west, and the south last. Then kneel down and pray, using the Lord's Name in vain again. Now you have turned your back on the world. Go home and you can do any evil you want to, for you have the devil on your side.

—SORCERER'S RITE

*I*n our several hundred years of enforced isolation in this country we have had plenty of time and plenty of reason to sing each other songs and tell each other tales.

—HALL JOHNSON

*I*t's bad luck to sweep trash from the house outside after sundown.

—TRADITIONAL

When you comb your hair, burn it up so won't nobody get it and work a root on you.

—GULLAH SUPERSTITION

My eye [is] itchin'. Company must be coming.

—AFRICAN-AMERICAN SAYING, SOURCE UNKNOWN

A new nail in an apple tree keeps the tree from being wormy.

—AFRICAN-AMERICAN SAYING, SOURCE UNKNOWN

To make grapes grow on vine, bury old shoes under vine. When shoes rot, grapes grow.

—AFRICAN-AMERICAN SAYING, SOURCE UNKNOWN

Cut some hair out of your man's head and put it in a jar in a hole under your step. That'll keep him coming.

—HOODOO CONJURE

I f you want to get rid of your boyfriend, take a picture and put it up face bottom in your shoe, and he'll fade away from you.

— FOLK REMEDY

F or dog bites, let dog lick it and it heals.

— FOLK REMEDY

P eel a onion and put it at the bottom of baby's feet for fever.

— FOLK REMEDY

Freedom/Liberty

W hen the Russian serfs had their chains broken and were given their liberty, the government of Russia—aye, the despotic government of Russia—gave to those poor emancipated serfs a few acres of land on which they would live and earn their bread.

But when you turned us loose, you gave us no acres. You turned us loose to the sky, to the storm, to the whirlwind, and, worst of all, you turned us loose to the wrath of our infuriated masters.

—FREDERICK DOUGLASS, 1876

... *t*he States where the largest measure of justice and civil rights has been granted to the colored man, both as to suffrage and his oath in court, are among the most rich, intelligent, enlightened and prosperous.

—FROM A PETITION TO THE TENNESSEE
CONSTITUTIONAL CONVENTION TO GRANT
AFRICAN AMERICANS THE RIGHT TO VOTE

... *f*or in every human Breast, God has implanted a Principle, which we call Love of Freedom; it is impatient of Oppression, and pants for Deliverance; and by the Leave of our Modern Egyptians I will assert, that the same Principle lives in us.

—PHILLIS WHEATLEY

*I*n every man's mind the good seeds of liberty are planted, and he who brings his fellow down so low, as to make him contented with a condition of slavery, commits the highest crime against God and man.

—HENRY HIGHLAND GARNET

. . . *i*ndependence is an essential condition of respectability.

—AN ADDRESS TO THE COLORED PEOPLE OF THE UNITED STATES FROM THE COLORED NATIONAL CONVENTION OF 1848

. . . *t*he liberty of a people is always insecure who have not absolute control of their own political destiny.

—DECLARATION OF THE PRINCIPLES OF THE NATIONAL EMIGRATION CONVENTION, 1854

*T*he humblest peasant is as free in the sight of God as the proudest monarch that ever swayed a sceptre. Liberty is a spirit sent from God, and like its great Author, is no respecter of persons.

—HENRY HIGHLAND GARNET

... *i* f we desire liberty, it can only be obtained at the price which others have paid for it.

—DECLARATION OF THE PRINCIPLES OF THE
NATIONAL EMIGRATION CONVENTION, 1854

*T*he caged lion may cease to roar, and try no longer the strength of the bars of his prison, and lie with his head between his mighty paws and snuff the polluted air, though he breathe not. But is he contented? Does he not instinctively long for the freedom of the forest and the plain? Yes, he is a lion still.

—HENRY HIGHLAND GARNET

*T*HE FUNERAL OF MARTIN LUTHER KING, JR.
His headstone said
Free at last, Free at last
But death is a slave's freedom
We seek the freedom of free men
And the construction of a world
Where Martin Luther King
    could have lived
        and preached nonviolence.

—NIKKI GIOVANNI

It's easy to be independent when you've got money. But to be independent when you haven't got a thing—that's the Lord's test.

— MAHALIA JACKSON

It may get me crucified, I may even die. But I want it said even if I die in the struggle that "He died to make men free."

— MARTIN LUTHER KING, JR.

Democracy itself is obstructed and stagnated to the extent that any of its channels are closed.

— ALAIN LOCKE

Oh freedom, oh freedom, oh freedom, over me
And before I'd be a slave, I'll be buried in my grave
And go home to my Lord and be free.

— TRADITIONAL SONG

I was free, but there was no one to welcome me to the land of freedom. I was a stranger in a strange land.

— HARRIET TUBMAN

f reedom is a state of mind: a spiritual unchoking of the wells of human power and superhuman love.

— W. E. B. Du Bois

f reedom is the most precious of our treasures, and it will not be allowed to vanish so long as men survive who offered their lives for it.

— Paul Robeson

f reedom was something internal. The outside signs were just signs and symbols of the man inside. All you could do was to give the opportunity for freedom and the man himself must make his own emancipation.

— Zora Neale Hurston

I t is only those who are free inside who can help those around them.

— Peter Abrahams

T he most rewarding freedom is freedom of the mind.

— Amy Garvey

A man is free or he is not. There cannot be any apprenticeship for freedom.

> —LeRoi Jones (Amiri Baraka)

The price of liberty is eternal vigilance.

> —Frederick Douglass

Freedom is not free.

> —Martin Luther King, Jr.

The price of freedom is death.

> —Malcolm X

Songs of liberation—who can lock them up? The spirit of freedom—who can jail it?

> —Paul Robeson

... *w* hite corn and yellow will mix by the taussels but the black and white Race must mix by the roots as they are so well mixed and has no taussels—freedom and liberty is the word with the Collored people ...

—FROM A LETTER BY A COLORED MAN TO
ABRAHAM LINCOLN, 1863

W e hold that freedom is the natural right of all men, which they themselves have no more right to give or barter away, than they have to sell their honor, their wives, or their children.

—FROM A PETITION TO THE TENNESSEE
CONSTITUTIONAL CONVENTION TO GRANT
AFRICAN AMERICANS THE RIGHT TO VOTE

A ll the nations of the earth are crying out for liberty and equality. Away, away with tyranny and oppression! And shall Africa's sons be silent any longer? Far be it from me to recommend to you either to kill, burn, or destroy. But I would strongly recommend to you to improve your talents; let not one lie buried in the earth. Show forth your powers of mind. Prove to the world that Though black your skins as shades of night, your hearts are pure, your souls are white.

—MARIA W. STEWART

... *t* his man [Malcolm X]
shall be remembered. O, not with statues' rhetoric,
not with legends and poems and wreaths of bronze alone,
but with the lives grown out of his life, the lives
fleshing his dream of the beautiful, needful thing.

—ROBERT HAYDEN

O n whatsoever soul Freedom may light, the course of that
soul is thenceforth onward and upward.

—JAMES McCUNE SMITH

D ear children, born in slavery but free at last! May God
preserve to you all the blessings of freedom and may you be
in every possible way fitted to enjoy them.

—CHARLOTTE FORTEN [GRIMKÉ]

F reedom always entails danger.

—W. E. B. DU BOIS

I know the bitterness of being accused and harassed by prosecutors. I know the horror of being hunted and haunted. I have dashed across continents and oceans as a fugitive, and have matched my wits with the police and secret agents seeking to deprive me of one of the greatest blessings man can have—liberty.

—JACK JOHNSON

*W*hen we let freedom ring, when we let it ring from every village and every hamlet, from every state and every city, we will be able to speed up that day when all of God's children, black men and white men, Jews and Gentiles, Protestants and Catholics, will be able to join hands and sing in the words of the old Negro spiritual, "Free at last! free at last! thank God almighty, we are free at last!"

—MARTIN LUTHER KING, JR.

Goals

... *n* o people ... can ever attain to greatness who lose their identity, as they must rise entirely upon their own native merits.

— DECLARATION OF THE PRINCIPLES OF THE
NATIONAL EMIGRATION CONVENTION, 1854

E very persecuted individual and race should get much consolation out of the great human law, which is universal and eternal, that merit, no matter under what skin found, is, in the long run, recognized and rewarded.

— BOOKER T. WASHINGTON

B e Black, shine, aim high.

— LEONTYNE PRICE

Blessed is the man who to himself has kept the high creations of his soul.

—ALEXANDER PUSHKIN

If a man hasn't discovered something that he will die for, he isn't fit to live.

—MARTIN LUTHER KING, JR.

Never in my life have I experienced utter despair. . . . Something in me has always been convinced that I am a child of great destiny, that I have a star, that I am led on by it toward great fulfillment.

—JEAN TOOMER

There is in this world no such force as the force of a man determined to rise.

—W. E. B. DU BOIS

An artist must be free to choose what he does, certainly, but he must also never be afraid to do what he might choose.

—LANGSTON HUGHES

We young Negro artists who create now intend to express our individual dark-skinned selves without fear or shame. If white people are pleased we are glad. If they are not, it doesn't matter. We know we are beautiful. And ugly too. The tom-tom cries and the tom-tom laughs. If colored people are pleased we are glad. If they are not, their displeasure doesn't matter either. We build our temples for tomorrow, strong as we know how, and we stand on top of the mountain, free within ourselves.

—LANGSTON HUGHES

Exercise the right to dream. You must face reality—that which is. But then dream of the reality that ought to be, that must be. Live beyond the pain of reality with the dream of a bright tomorrow. Use hope and imagination as weapons of survival and progress. Use love to motivate you and obligate you to serve the human family.

—JESSE JACKSON

We will build a democratic America in spite of undemocratic Americans. We have rarely worried about the odds or the obstacles before—we will not start worrying now. We will have both of our goals—Peace and Power!

—SHIRLEY CHISHOLM

A goal that is the basis of true democracy above the law: A child born to a Black mother in a state like Mississippi —born to the dumbest, poorest sharecropper—by merely drawing its first breath in the democracy has exactly the same rights as a white baby born to the wealthiest person in the United States. It's not true, but I challenge anyone to say it is not a goal worth working for.

— THURGOOD MARSHALL

D id you ever have a goal and still not know where you're going? I knew I wasn't going to stay where I was but I wasn't sure just where I was going.

— JOE LOUIS

N ever give up. Keep your thoughts and your mind always on the goal.

— TOM BRADLEY

B eing a runner was my biggest goal. Now I'm the fastest woman in the world on a track.

— EVELYN ASHFORD

I was . . . silenced solely because cadets did not want Blacks at West Point. Their only purpose was to freeze me out. What they did not realize was that I was stubborn enough to put up with their treatment to reach the goal I had come to attain.

—BENJAMIN DAVIS, JR.

To the tired climbers, the horizon was ever dark, the mists were often cold, the Canaan was always dim and far away.

—W. E. B. DU BOIS

Our strength is that with the total society saying to us, "NO, NO, NO, NO," we continue to move toward our goal.

—RALPH ELLISON

God

Our Fader which art in heaben,
White man owe me eleben and pay me seben.
D'y kingdom come, d'y will be done,
If I hadn't tuck dat I wouldn't git none.

—FROM A SLAVE RHYME

God'll let you fly when He gives you wings up in heaven.

—RICHARD WRIGHT

God made everything to pass and perish except stones. God made stones for memory. He builds a mountain Himself when He wants things not forgot. Then His voice is heard in rumbling judgment.

—ZORA NEALE HURSTON

We have no Property! We have no Wives! No Children! We have no City! No Country! But we have a Father in Heaven, and we are determined as far as his Grace shall enable us, and as far as our degraded contemptuous Life will admit, to keep all his Commandments. . . .

—PETITION OF THE AFRICANS LIVING IN BOSTON,
1773

Some of these mornings bright and fair,
I thank God I'm free at last,
Going to meet my Jesus in the middle of the air,
I thank God I'm free at last.

—SPIRITUAL

God gives nothing to those who keep their arms crossed.
—AFRICAN PROVERB

One and God make a majority.
—FREDERICK DOUGLASS

'T want me, 'twas the Lord. I always told Him, "I trust you. I don't know where to go or what to do, but I expect you to lead me." And he always did.

— HARRIET TUBMAN

I have always thanked God for making me a man, but Martin Delany always thanked God for making him a black man.

— FREDERICK DOUGLASS

My chief problem has been that of reconciling a Christian upbringing with a pagan inclination.

— COUNTEE CULLEN

And then last night, I tiptoed up
To my daughter's room and heard her
Talking to someone, and when I opened
The door, there was no one there . . .
Only she on her knees, peeking into
Her own clasped hands.

— LEROI JONES (AMIRI BARAKA)

God punishes the indifference of men who remain cold and proud before the terrible spectacles He presents to them.

—ALEXANDRE DUMAS

Every race of people since time began who have attempted to describe God by words or painting, or by carvings, have conveyed the idea that the God who made them and shaped their destinies was symbolized in themselves, and why should not the Negro believe that he resembles God as much as other people?

—HENRY MCNEAL TURNER

God made us men long before man made us citizens.

—CHARLES T. WALKER

Black men are not going to cringe before anyone but God.

—MARCUS GARVEY

Young man—
Young man—
Your arm's too short to box with God.

—JAMES WELDON JOHNSON

God is a means of liberation and not a means to control others.

—JAMES BALDWIN

I cannot see everything, but nothing escapes God.

—TOUSSAINT L'OUVERTURE

In the midst of lonely days and dreary nights I have heard an inner voice saying, "Lo, I will be with you."

—MARTIN LUTHER KING, JR.

God is man idealized.

—LEROI JONES (AMIRI BARAKA)

*M*an lives in God, and the circumference of life cannot be rightly drawn until the center is set.

—BENJAMIN E. MAYS

*W*e live inside this unbelievable cosmos, inside our unbelievable bodies—everything so perfect, everything so in tune. I got to think God had a hand in it.

—RAY CHARLES

*I*n the beginning God, . . . in the end God.

—DESMOND TUTU

I do not know which of our afflictions God intends that we overcome and which He means for us to bear.

—JEAN TOOMER

*T*here isn't a certain time we should set aside to talk about God. God is part of our every waking moment.

—MARVA COLLINS

Give it for the sake of God and give it even to him who does not believe in God.

—BENIN PROVERB

God made the sea, we make the ship; He made the wind, we make a sail; He made the calm, we make oars.

—SENEGAL PROVERB

A something said within my breast, "Press forward, I will be with thee." And my heart made this reply, "Lord, if thou wilt be with me, then I will speak for thee as long as I live."

—MARIA W. STEWART

Descendant of slave and of slave owner, I had already been called poet, lawyer, teacher, and friend. Now I was empowered to minister the sacrament of One in whom there is no north or south, no black or white, or male or female—only the spirit of love and reconciliation drawing us all to-ward the goal of human wholeness.

—PAULI MURRAY

I am a poor pilgrim of sorrow. . . .
I'm tryin' to make heaven my home.
Sometimes I am tossed and driven.
Sometimes I don't know where to roam.
I've heard of a city called heaven.
I've started to make it my home.

—TRADITIONAL SPIRITUAL

*D*ust, dust and ashes, fly over my grave,
But the Lord shall bear my spirit home.

—TRADITIONAL SONG

Happiness

*D*e harder me cross to bear down here de better I go be prepare to tek me place in dat Happy Land where all is 'joicin, an' when I git dere, I want de Lord to say, ". . . come an' rest wid de elect ob de Lord!"

—GULLAH TRADITIONAL

T reat us like men, and there is no danger but we will all live in peace and happiness together.

—DAVID WALKER

E xhaust the little moment. Soon it dies.
And be it gash or gold it will not come
Again in this identical disguise.

—GWENDOLYN BROOKS

[T] here is neither happiness nor unhappiness in this world; there is only the comparison of one state with another.

—ALEXANDRE DUMAS

H appiness is perfume, you can't pour it on somebody else without getting a few drops on yourself.

—JAMES VAN DER ZEE

There must always be the continuing struggle to make the increasing knowledge of the world bear some fruit in increasing understanding and in the production of human happiness.

—CHARLES R. DREW

People who make a living doing something they don't enjoy wouldn't even be happy with a one-day work week.

—DUKE ELLINGTON

The Declaration of Independence declares the right of life, liberty, and the pursuit of happiness. The catch is that it doesn't give you the chance to catch up with happiness.

—NATHAN HARE, JR.

My concept of happiness is to be fulfilled in a spiritual sense.

—CORETTA SCOTT KING

*H*appiness can grow from only a little contentment.

— PYGMY PROVERB

*S*uch is the quiet bless [bliss] of soul,
　　When in some calm retreat
Where pensive thoughts like streamlets roll,
　　And render silence sweet.

— GEORGE MOSES HORTON

*O*h, ye pleasure-seeking sons and daughters of idleness, who move with measured step, listless and snail-like through the slow-winding cotillion; if ye wish to look upon the celerity, if not the "poetry of motion," upon genuine happiness rampant and unrestrained, go down to Louisiana and see the slaves dancing in the starlight of a Christmas night.

— SOLOMON NORTHUP

*T*he white man's happiness cannot be purchased by the black man's misery.

— FREDERICK DOUGLASS

*H*ate

*W*it, ridicule, false philosophy, and an impure theology, with a flood of low black-guardism, come through this channel into the public mind; constantly feeding and keeping alive against us, the bitterest hate.

— AN ADDRESS TO THE COLORED PEOPLE OF THE UNITED STATES FROM THE COLORED NATIONAL CONVENTION OF 1848

*W*hen you clench your fist, no one can put anything in your hand, nor can your hand pick up anything.

— ALEX HALEY

*H*atred, which could destroy so much, never failed to destroy the man who hated and this is an immutable law.

— JAMES BALDWIN

Hatred is one long wait.

—RENÉ MARAN

Those who become inoculated with the virus of race hatred are more unfortunate than the victim of it. Race hatred is the most malignant poison that can afflict the mind. It freezes up the fount of inspiration and chills the higher faculties of the soul.

—KELLY MILLER

What do you get out of hating people, out of having this bitterness in your heart always?

—PETER ABRAHAMS

Men often hate each other because they fear each other; they fear each other because they do not know each other; they do not know each other because they cannot communicate; they cannot communicate because they are separated.

—A. PHILIP RANDOLPH

When you have taught a man to hate himself, you've really got it and gone.

—MALCOLM X

Men must be carefully taught to hate, and the lessons learned by one generation must be relearned by the next.

—LERONE BENNETT, JR.

The price of hating other human beings is loving oneself less.

—ELDRIDGE CLEAVER

Only those who permit themselves to be, are despised.

—ALEX HALEY

Hating you shall be a game
Played with cool hands
And slim fingers.

—GWENDOLYN BENNETT

*H*atred shook her as a strong wind shakes a boughless tree.

—J. SAUNDERS REDDING

... *t*here is, I should think, no Negro living in America who has not felt, briefly or for long periods, with anguish sharp or dull, in varying degrees and to varying effect, simple, naked and unanswerable hatred. . . .

—JAMES BALDWIN

Heritage

*I*t is not skin color which makes a Negro American but cultural heritage as shaped by the American experience, the social and political predicament.

—RALPH ELLISON

*E*very generation needs the instruction and insights of past generations in order to forge its own vision.

—JESSE JACKSON

We are one people—one in general complexion, one in a common degradation, one in popular estimation. As one rises, all must rise, and as one falls all must fall.

—An Address to the Colored People of the United States from the Colored National Convention of 1848

The influence of ancestry, however, is important in helping forward any individual or race, if too much reliance is not placed upon it.

—Booker T. Washington

O black and unknown bards of long ago,
How came your lips to touch the sacred fire?
How, in your darkness, did you come to know
The power and beauty of the minstrel's lyre?

—James Weldon Johnson

We, today, stand on the shoulders of our predecessors who have gone before us. We, as their successors, must catch the torch of freedom and liberty passed on to us by our ancestors. We cannot lose in this battle.

— BENJAMIN E. MAYS

For it means something to be a Negro, after all, as it means something to have been born in Ireland or in China, to live where one sees space and sky or to live where one sees nothing but rubble or nothing but high buildings.

— JAMES BALDWIN

We were here before the Anglo-Saxon evolved, and thick lips and heavy lidded eyes looked out from the inscrutable face of the sphinx across the sands of Egypt, while yet the ancestors of those who now oppress him were practicing human sacrifices and painting themselves with wood and the Negro is here yet.

— CHARLES W. CHESNUTT

I am where I am because of the bridges that I crossed. Sojourner Truth was a bridge. Harriet Tubman was a bridge. Ida B. Wells was a bridge. Madame C. J. Walker was a bridge. Fannie Lou Hamer was a bridge.

—OPRAH WINFREY

*N*ot to know what one's race has done in former times is to continue always a child.

—CARTER G. WOODSON

*W*e will win our freedom because the sacred heritage of our nation and the eternal will of God are embodied in our echoing demands.

—MARTIN LUTHER KING, JR.

*W*e cannot escape our origins, however hard we try, those origins which contain the key—could we but find it—to all that we later become.

—JAMES BALDWIN

We must recapture our heritage and our ideals if we are to liberate ourselves from the bonds of white supremacy. We must launch a cultural revolution to unbrainwash an entire people.

—MALCOLM X

Like jars of ginger we are sealed
By nature's heritage.

—GWENDOLYN BENNETT

Histories are important 'cause they point the direction of traditions.

—NIKKI GIOVANNI

Sociologists often assert that there is a Negro thing—a timbre of a voice, a style, a rhythm—in all of its positive and negative implications, the expression of a certain kind of American uniqueness. . . . If there is this uniqueness, why on earth would it not in some way be precious to the people who maintain it?

—RALPH ELLISON

. . . one group advocates embracing the riches of the folk heritage; their opposites demand a clean break with the past and all it represents. Had I not gone home summers and hobnobbed with Negroes, I would have finished college without knowing that any Negro other than Paul Laurence Dunbar ever wrote a poem. I would have come out imagining that the story of the Negro could be told in two short paragraphs: a statement about jungle people in Africa and an equally brief account of the slavery issue in American history.

— ARNA BONTEMPS

. . . we black men seem the sole oasis of simple faith and reverence in a dusty desert of dollars and smartness.

— W. E. B. DU BOIS

Wherever the Negro face appears a tension is created, the tension of a silence filled with things unutterable.

— JAMES BALDWIN

. . . there was a world in which you wore your everyday clothes on Sunday, and there was a world in which you wore your Sunday clothes every day . . .

— RALPH ELLISON

[On the Middle Passage:]
One day we had a smooth sea and moderate wind, two of my countrymen were chained together (I was near them at the time), preferring death to such a life of misery, somehow made through nettings and jumped into the sea; immediately another quite dejected fellow, who, on account of his illness, was suffered to be out of irons, also followed their example; and I believe many more would very soon have done the same if they had not been prevented by the ship's crew. . . .

— OLAUDAH EQUIANO

We are no more aliens to this country or to its institutions than our brothers in white. We have instituted it; our forefathers paid dearly for it. The broken hearts of those who first landed here is the first price that was paid for the blessings for which we now contend. By the God of right, by the God of justice, by the God of love, we will stay here and enjoy it, share and share alike with those who call us aliens, and invite us to go. Together we planted the tree of liberty and watered its roots with our tears and blood, and under its branches we will stay and be sheltered.

— THOMAS EZEKIEL MILLER

One cannot give to a person that which he already possesses.

— TOUSSAINT L'OUVERTURE

I leave you love.

— MARY MCLEOD BETHUNE

My father was a slave, and my people died to build this country, and I am going to stay and have a piece of it just like you.

— PAUL ROBESON

We read the future by the past.

— ALEXANDER CRUMMELL

There is no prejudice against color among the slaveholders. Their social system and one million mulattoes are facts which no arguments can demolish.

— JOHN S. ROCK

*H*onor

*I*f you must bleed, let it come all at once—rather *die freemen, than live to be slaves.*

— HENRY HIGHLAND GARNET

*I*f you knew him you would know why we must honor him: Malcolm was our manhood, our living black manhood! This was his meaning to his people. And, in honoring him, we honor the best in ourselves. . . . Consigning these mortal remains to earth, the common mother of all, secure in the knowledge that what we place in the ground is no more now a man—but a seed—which, after the winter of our discontent will come forth again to meet us. And we will know him then for what he was and is—a Prince—our own black shining Prince!—who didn't hesitate to die, because he loved us so.

— OSSIE DAVIS

We shall have our manhood. We shall have it or the earth will be leveled by our attempts to gain it.

— ELDRIDGE CLEAVER

A jam session is a polite encounter, or an exchange of compliments, but in the old days they had cutting contests, where you defended your honor with your instrument.

— DUKE ELLINGTON

Never give in, never, never, never—in nothing great or small, large or petty—never give in—except in convictions of honor and good sense.

— TOM BRADLEY

What is the colored men fighting for if the[y] makes us free we are happy to hear it And when we are free men and a people we will fight for our rights and liberty we care nothing about the union we heave been in it Slaves over two undred And fifty years we have made the contry and So far Saved the union and if we heave to fight for our rights let us fight under Colored officers for we are the men that will kill the Enemies of the Government

— FROM A LETTER BY A BLACK MAN TO
ABRAHAM LINCOLN, 1863

It is only what is written upon the soul of man that will survive the wreck of time.

—FRANCIS JAMES GRIMKÉ

Everywhere I go, I'm being honored and I don't really deserve it. It makes me scared.

—MUHAMMAD ALI

Hope

Hope is the pillar of the world.

—AFRICAN PROVERB

I ask no monument, proud and high,
To arrest the gaze of the passers-by;
All that my yearning spirit craves,
Is bury me not in a land of slaves.

—FRANCES ELLEN WATKINS HARPER

Go down, Moses,
Way down in Egypt land
Tell old Pharaoh
To let my people go.

— SPIRITUAL

I'm here, I exist and there's hope.

— VERNON JARRETT

Someday the sun is going to shine down on me in some
faraway place.

— MAHALIA JACKSON

What one hopes for is better than what one finds.

— AFRICAN PROVERB

Through the children of to-day we believe we can build
the foundation of the next generation upon such a rock of
morality, intelligence and strength, that the floods of pro-
scription, prejudice and persecution may descend upon it in
torrents and yet it will not be moved.

— MARY CHURCH TERRELL

[T] here are three things I was born with in this world, and there are three things I will have until the day I die: hope, determination, and song.

— MIRIAM MAKEBA

[O] ut of the sighs of one generation are kneaded the hopes of the next.

— JOAQUIN MACHADO DE ASSIS

[I] have the audacity to believe that people everywhere can have three meals a day for their bodies, education and culture for their minds, and dignity, equality and freedom for their spirits. I believe that what self-centered men have torn down men other-centered can build up. I still believe that one day mankind will bow before the altars of God and be crowned triumphant over war and bloodshed, and non-violent redemptive goodwill proclaim the rule of the land.

— MARTIN LUTHER KING, JR.

[I] t is easy to be hopeful in the day when you can see the things you wish on.

— ZORA NEALE HURSTON

*H*ope is a delicate suffering.

—LeRoi Jones (Amiri Baraka)

I have a dream that one day this nation will rise up and live out the true meaning of its creed: "We hold these truths to be self-evident; that all men are created equal."

I have a dream that one day on the red hills of Georgia the sons of former slaves and the sons of former slaveowners will be able to sit down together at the table of brotherhood. . . .

I have a dream that my four little children will one day live in a nation where they will not be judged by the color of their skin but by the content of their character. . . .

I have a dream today.

I have a dream that one day every valley shall be exalted, every hill and mountain shall be made low, the rough places will be made plains, and the crooked places will be made straight, and the glory of the Lord shall be revealed, and all flesh shall see it together.

—Martin Luther King, Jr.

*W*here there is hope there is life, where there is life there is possibility and where there is possibility change can occur.

—Jesse Jackson

Oh! that I had the wings of a dove, that I might soar away to where there is no slavery; no clanking of chains, no captives, no lacerating of backs, no parting of husbands and wives; and where man ceases to be the property of his fellow man.

—HENRY BIBB

With tow'ring hopes, and growing grace arise . . .

—PHILLIS WHEATLEY

Let us all hope that the dark clouds of racial prejudice will soon pass away and the deep fog of misunderstanding will be lifted from our fear-drenched communities and in some not too distant tomorrow the radiant stars of love and brotherhood will shine over our great nation with all their scintillating beauty.

—MARTIN LUTHER KING, JR.

Swing low, sweet chariot,
Coming for to carry me home. . . .

—TRADITIONAL SPIRITUAL

When the Lord said, "Let there be light," and there was light, what I want to know is where was us colored people?

—LANGSTON HUGHES

My soul wants something that's new, that's new . . .

—TRADITIONAL SONG

Every time they strike us, they strikin' Your Son;
Every time they shove us in, they cornerin' they own children.
I'm gonna scream before I hope again.
I ain't never gonna hush my mouth or lay down this heavy,
    black, weary, terrible load
Until I fights to stamp my feet with my black sons
On a freedom solid rock and stand there peaceful
And look out into the star wilderness of the sky
And the land lyin' about clean, and secure land,
And people not afraid again.

—OWEN DODSON

*H*umor

H umor is when the joke is on you but hits the other fellow first—because it boomerangs. Humor is what you wish in your secret heart were not funny, but it is, and you must laugh. Humor is your unconscious therapy.

— LANGSTON HUGHES

I 've got to be a colored funny man, not a funny colored man.

— DICK GREGORY

"*Y* ou scoundrel, you ate my turkey," the master admonishes.

"Yes, suh, Massa, you got less turkey but you sho nuff got mo' Nigger," the slave replies.

— SLAVE FOLKLORE

We couldn't escape, so we developed a style of humor which recognized the basic artificiality, the irrationality, of the actual arrangement.

—RALPH ELLISON

"Sorry, we don't serve colored folks here." His reply, "Fine, I don't eat them, just bring me a medium rare hamburger."

—DICK GREGORY

"Pompey, how do I look?" the master asked.
"O, massa, mighty. You looks mighty."
"What do you mean 'Mighty,' Pompey?"
"Why, massa, you looks noble."
"What do you mean by noble?"
"Why, suh, you looks just like a lion."
"Why, Pompey, where have you ever seen a lion?"
"I saw one down in yonder field the other day, massa."
"Pompey, you foolish fellow, that was a jackass."
"Was it, massa? Well, suh, you looks just like him."

—PETER RANDOLPH

This was the piquant flavoring to the national joke, it lay behind our benevolence: Aunt Jemima and Uncle Tom, our creations, at the last had evaded us; they had a life—their own, perhaps a better life than ours—and they would never tell us what it was.

— JAMES BALDWIN

If God ever wanted my mouth any bigger, he would have to move my ears.

— BILLY KERSANDS

All the jokes in the world are based on a few elemental ideas. The sight of other people in trouble is nearly always funny.

— BERT WILLIAMS

My father said, "The garbage man is here," and my mother said, "Ask him to leave a couple of bags."

— REDD FOXX

*A*n old man can't do nothing for me but bring me a message from a young one.

— MOMS MABLEY

I was on my way down to Miami . . . I mean They-ami. I was ridin' along in my Cadillac, you know, goin' through one of them little towns in South Carolina. Pass through a red light. One of them big cops come runnin' over to me, say, "Hey, woman, don't you know you went through a red light?" I say, "Yeah, I know I went through a red light." "Well, what did you do that for?" I said, " 'Cause I seen all you white folks goin' on the green light . . . thought the red light was for us!"

— MOMS MABLEY

*Y*ou get a couple of preachers, the next step is to have a bunch a honky social workers. Next thing you know they done fixed the street, put in new sewers, built a new school, an' raised the taxes. There goes the damn neighborhood.

— DAVID BRADLEY (SOUTH STREET snaps)

*N*obody laughs at the miseries of life like the Negro. He accepts things, not with resignation but with amusement. . . . How could you wound a fellow who simply laughed? How could you be sure what he was laughing at? Himself? Maybe. But I know I'd begin to think he might be laughing at me.

—RUDOLPH FISHER

*W*hen they call you nigger to make a rhyme with trigger it makes the gun backfire.

—RALPH ELLISON

*N*iggers just have a way of telling you stuff and not telling you stuff. Martians would have a difficult time with Niggers. They be translating words, saying a whole lot of things underneath you, all around you . . . that's our comedy.

—RICHARD PRYOR

A woman is a woman until the day she dies, but a man's a man only as long as he can.

—MOMS MABLEY

White people, quit moving around the country like a bunch of damned gypsies. Wherever you are, we'll be there.

— REDD FOXX

Used to be some beautiful black men would come through the neighborhood dressed in African shit, really nice shit. And they be . . . "Peace, love, black is beautiful, remember the essence of life, we are a people of the universe, life is beautiful." My parents would go, "That nigger crazy."

— RICHARD PRYOR

You gotta say this for whites, their self-confidence knows no bounds. Who else could go to a small island in the South Pacific, where there's no crime, poverty, unemployment, war, or worry—and call it a "primitive society."

— DICK GREGORY

There's a thin line between to laugh with and to laugh at.

— RICHARD PRYOR

She don't look lak a thing but a hunk uh liver wid hair on it.

—ZORA NEALE HURSTON

If ugliness were bricks, your mother would be a housing project.

—THE DOZENS

You're so dumb, you think Beirut was a famous home-run hitter.

—THE DOZENS

You're so stupid, on the job application where it said "Sign here," you wrote "Aquarius."

—THE DOZENS

Your ears are so big, you can hear sign language.

—THE DOZENS

...*A*merica is such a paradoxical society, hypocritically paradoxical, that if you don't have some humor, you'll crack up.

—MALCOLM X

*H*umor is laughing at what you haven't got when you ought to have it.

—LANGSTON HUGHES

*H*umor cleanses the heart and keeps it good.

—ALFRED PASTER

*J*oy is finding a pregnant roach
and squashing it.

—NIKKI GIOVANNI

*D*e price of yo' hat ain't de measure of yo' brain.

—PROVERB

I*dentity*

I find, in being black, a thing of beauty: a joy; a strength; a secret cup of gladness—a native land in neither time nor place—a native land in every Negro face! Be loyal to your-selves: your skin; your hair; your lips, your southern speech, your laughing kindness—are Negro kingdoms, vast as any other.

—OSSIE DAVIS

The American image of the Negro lives also in the Negro's heart; and when he has surrendered to this image life has no other possible reality.

—JAMES BALDWIN

We are the only human beings in the world with fifty seven variety of complexions who are classed together as a single racial unit.

—MARY CHURCH TERRELL

I t is a peculiar sensation, this double-consciousness, this sense of always looking at one's self through the eyes of others, of measuring one's soul by the tape of a world that looks on in amused contempt and pity. One ever feels his twoness—an American, a Negro; two souls, two thoughts, two unreconciled strivings; two warring ideals in one dark body.

— W. E. B. Du Bois

O nce you know who you are, you don't have to worry any more.

— Nikki Giovanni

O ne may say that the Negro in America does not really exist except in the darkness of our minds.

— James Baldwin

W e live surrounded by white images, and white in this world is synonymous with the good, light, beauty, success, so that, despite ourselves sometimes, we run after that whiteness and deny our darkness, which has been made into the symbol of all that is evil or inferior.

— Paule Marshall

$\mathcal{A}$ dvice to Negro writers: Step *outside yourself*, then look back—and you will see how human, yet how beautiful and black you are. How very black—even when you're integrated.

— LANGSTON HUGHES

$\mathcal{G}$ ot one mind for white folk to see
'Nother for what I know is me.

— FROM A SLAVE NARRATIVE

$\mathcal{W}$ hite Boy,
the Negro dish is a mix
like . . . and *un*like
pimiento bisque, chop suey,
eggs à la Goldenrod, and eggaroni;
tongue-and-corn casserole, mulligan stew,
baked fillets of halibut, and cheese fondue;
macaroni milanaise, egg-milk shake,
mullagatawny soup, and sour-milk cake.

Just as the Chinese lack
an ideogram for "to be,"
our lexicon has no definition
for an ethnic amalgam like Black Boy and me.

— MELVIN B. TOLSON

*I*gnorance

*I*gnorance, my brethren, is a mist, low down into the very dark and almost impenetrable abyss in which our fathers for many centuries have been plunged.

— DAVID WALKER

*T*he lack of knowledge is darker than night.

— AFRICAN SAYING

*N*o human folly can surpass the conceit of ignorance.

— CHARLES V. ROMAN

*T*he ignorant are always prejudiced and the prejudiced are always ignorant.

— CHARLES V. ROMAN

*I*ntolerance can only grow in the soil of ignorance: from its branches grow all manner of obstacles to human progress.

— WALTER WHITE

*T*he realization of ignorance is the first act of knowing.

— JEAN TOOMER

*T*he eye sees; the mind understands.

— IBUZA PROVERB

*I*t used to be thought that ignorant negroes were the most valuable, but this belief probably originated from the fact that it is almost impossible to retain an educated, intelligent man in bondage.

— FROM A PETITION TO THE TENNESSEE CONSTITUTIONAL CONVENTION TO GRANT AFRICAN AMERICANS THE RIGHT TO VOTE

I t is the brutal, degraded, ignorant man who is usually the criminal.

> —FROM A PETITION TO THE TENNESSEE
> CONSTITUTIONAL CONVENTION TO GRANT
> AFRICAN AMERICANS THE RIGHT TO VOTE

Y ou know right there he was a lightweight fool.

> —J. CALIFORNIA COOPER

F or my people blundering and groping and floundering in the dark of churches and schools and clubs and societies, associations and councils and committees and conventions, distressed and disturbed and deceived and devoured by money-hungry glory-craving leeches, preyed on by facile force of state and fad and novelty, by false prophet and holy believer . . .

> —MARGARET WALKER

*J*ustice

I believe this is God's island, and ultimately He will make it right.

— STEVIE WONDER

G od writes national judgments upon national sins, and what may be slumbering in the storehouse of divine justice we do not know.

— FRANCES ELLEN WATKINS HARPER

... *t* here comes a time when the veriest worm will turn, and the Negro feels to-day that after all the work he has done, all the sacrifices he has made, and all the suffering he has endured, if he did not, now, defend his name and manhood from this vile accusation, he would be unworthy even of the contempt of mankind. It is to this charge he now feels he must make answer.

—W. E. B. DU BOIS

T rue peace is not merely the absence of tension but the presence of justice and brotherhood.

—MARTIN LUTHER KING, JR.

D isfranchisement is the deliberate theft and robbery of the only protection of poor against rich and black against white. The land that disfranchises its citizens and calls itself a democracy lies and knows it lies.

—CRISIS, MAY 1919

With courage born of success achieved in the past, with a keen sense of responsibility which we must continue to assume we look forward to the future, large with promise and hope. Seeking no favors because of our color or patronage because of our needs, we knock at the bar of justice and ask for an equal chance.

—MARY CHURCH TERRELL

. . . there is no justice except strength.

—MARCUS GARVEY

. . . we've come to cash this check, a check that will give us upon demand the riches of freedom and the security of justice.

—MARTIN LUTHER KING, JR.

To demand freedom is to demand justice. When there is no justice in the land, a man's freedom is threatened. Freedom and justice are interdependent. When a man has no protection under the law it is difficult for him to make others recognize him.

—JAMES CONE

Just like you can buy grades of silk, you can buy grades of justice.

— RAY CHARLES

The wrongdoer may forget but the wronged has a longer memory.

— AKAN PROVERB

To take revenge is often to sacrifice oneself.

— TERIK PROVERB

After two hundred years of bondage and suffering a returning sense of justice has awakened the great body of the American people to make amends for the unprovoked wrongs committed against us. . . .

— FROM A PETITION TO THE TENNESSEE CONSTITUTIONAL CONVENTION TO GRANT AFRICAN AMERICANS THE RIGHT TO VOTE

The boys guffawed, and Justice began to laugh
Like a maniac on a broken phonograph.
Bartender, make it straight and make it three—
One for the Negro . . . one for you and me.

— MELVIN B. TOLSON

Oh, how can we forget
Our human rights denied?
Oh, how can we forget
Our manhood crucified?
When Justice is profaned
And plea with curse is met,
When Freedom's gates are barred,
Oh, how can we forget?

— MELVIN B. TOLSON

Sorrow follows the footsteps of crime,
And Sin is the consort of Woe.

— FRANCES ELLEN WATKINS HARPER

I njustice anywhere is a threat to justice everywhere. We are caught in an inescapable network of mutuality, tied in a single garment of destiny. Whatever affects one directly affects all indirectly.

—MARTIN LUTHER KING, JR.

*K*nowledge

T o ask well is to know much.

—AFRICAN PROVERB

T here comes a point when you really have to spend time with yourself to know who you are. Black people need to be with ourselves.

—BERNICE JOHNSON REAGON

K nowledge of one's identity, one's self, community, nation, religion and God, is the true meaning of resurrection, while ignorance of it signifies hell.

—ELIJAH MUHAMMAD

Knowledge is better than riches.

—CAMEROONIAN SAYING

Knowledge is like a garden; if it is not cultivated, it cannot be harvested.

—GUINEAN SAYING

As one man learns from another, so nation learns from nation.

—WILLIAM WELLS-BROWN

Man cannot live without some knowledge of the purpose of life. If he can find no purpose in life he creates one in the inevitability of death.

—CHESTER B. HIMES

Armed with the knowledge of our past, we can with confidence charter a course for our future.

—MALCOLM X

A man without knowledge of himself and his heritage is like a tree without roots.

— DICK GREGORY

I f ignorance, poverty and degradation have hitherto been our unhappy lot; has the Eternal decree gone forth, that our race alone are to remain in this state, while knowledge and civilization are shedding their enlivening rays over the rest of the human family?

— EDITORIAL FROM THE FIRST EDITION OF
FREEDOM'S JOURNAL

T hey who humble themselves before knowledge of any kind generally end up the wiser and as voices with something meaningful to say.

— HAKI MADHUBUTI

W hen a man gains knowledge through the observation of the truth, his view of the world changes.

— KILINDI IYI

*Y*our husband may leave you, but what you have in your mind will never leave you.

—MIRIAM MAKEBA

*K*nowledge is not power, it is only potential power that becomes real through use.

—DOROTHY RILEY

*H*ow can human experience transcend humanity? It's the same thing.

—MARGARET WALKER

*W*onders do not confuse. We call them that
And close the matter there. But common things
Surprise us.

—GWENDOLYN BROOKS

*L*oneliness

M arried loneliness . . . call it what you will. You communicate all day with small children; you find yourself living for the evening and adult companionship and when it comes . . . it wants to be alone.

—VELMA POLLARD

L oneliness is random; solitude is ritual.

—PEARL CLEAGE

I always felt a sense of cosmic companionship. So that the loneliness and fear have faded away because of a greater feeling of security.

—MARTIN LUTHER KING, JR.

*I*t's a very lonely thing to be one of the first.

—ARTHUR MITCHELL

. . . *l*oneliness I wear like a torn coat. . . .

—LANCE JEFFERS

*L*ove

*T*he Queen of Sheba was an Ethiopian just like Jethro, with power unequal to man. She didn't have to deny herself to give gold to Solomon. She had gold-making words. But she was thirsty, and the country where she lived was dry to her mouth. So she listened to her talking ring and went to see Solomon, and the fountain in his garden quenched her thirst.

—ZORA NEALE HURSTON

Don't never go looking for love, girl. Just wait. It'll come. Like the rain fallin' from the heaven, it'll come. Just don't never give up on love.

—ZULU [NWAZULU] SOFOLA

When you see me leavin,
　　Hang yo haid an cry, Lawd, Lawd,
When you see me leavin,
　　Hang yo haid an cry.
Gonna love you
　　Til the day I die.

—TRADITIONAL FOLK SONG

Love without esteem cannot go far or reach high. It is an angel with only one wing.

—ALEXANDRE DUMAS, FILS

Never love with all your heart,
It only ends in aching;
And bit by bit to the smallest part
That organ will be breaking.

—COUNTEE CULLEN

*H*atred and bitterness can never cure the disease of fear, only love can do that. Hatred paralyzes life; love releases it. Hatred confuses life; love harmonizes it. Hatred darkens life; love illuminates it.

— MARTIN LUTHER KING, JR.

*I*ntellect and brain and academics are fine, but we also have a heart and soul, it is OK to use all aspects of ourselves.

— DOROTHY COTTON

*H*eaven and earth! How is it that bodies join but never meet?

— BEAH RICHARDS

*B*ENEDICTION
May hills lean toward you,
Hills and windswept mountains,
And trees be happy
That have seen you pass.

— DONALD JEFFREY HAYES

*L*ove is like a baby, it needs to be treated gently.

— CONGOLESE SAYING

*L*et your love be like the misty rains, coming softly, but flooding the river.

— SAYING OF MADAGASCAR

*I*t is better to be loved than feared.

— SENEGALESE SAYING

I could love her with a love so warm
You could not break it with a fairy charm;
I could love her with a love so bold
It would not die, e'en tho' the world grew cold.

— FENTON JOHNSON

*M*y love is dark as yours is fair,
Yet lovelier I hold her
Than listless maids with pallid hair,
And blood that's thin and colder.

— COUNTEE CULLEN

When you love a man, he becomes more than a body. His physical limbs expand, and his outline recedes, vanishes. He is rich and sweet and right. He is part of the world, the atmosphere, the blue sky and the blue water.

— GWENDOLYN BROOKS

Love, like electricity or revolution or becoming, is a process (not a thing).

— AL YOUNG

Unconditional love not only means I am with you, but also I am for you, all the way, right or wrong. . . . Love is indescribable and unconditional. I could tell you a thousand things that it is not, but not one that it is. Either you have it or you haven't, there's no proof of it.

— DUKE ELLINGTON

Or maybe the purpose of being here, wherever we are, is to increase the durability and the occasions of love among and between peoples. Love, as the concentration of tender caring and tender excitement, or love as the reason for joy. . . .

— JUNE JORDAN

The less one loves a woman, the surer one is of possessing her.

—ALEXANDER PUSHKIN

I am a woman and you are a man and I have always known it. If you love me, tell me so. Don't approach me as you would an enemy. I am on your side and have always been. We have survived, and we may just be able to teach the world a lesson.

—FRAN SANDERS

... Only death can rob me of my will to love the one I love.

—JOSHUA HENRY JONES

[Love makes your] soul crawl out from its hiding place.

—ZORA NEALE HURSTON

Romance without finance is no good.

—WILLIE ''THE LION'' SMITH

*D*on't threaten me with love, baby. Let's go walking in the rain.

— BILLIE HOLIDAY

*L*ove has no awareness of merit or demerit; it has no scale by which its portion may be weighed or measured. It does not seek to balance giving and receiving. Love loves; this is its nature.

— HOWARD THURMAN

*P*erhaps it was more happiness than love, though the one cannot exist without the other. . . . Happiness and passion. Maybe that is what love really is.

— CAMARA LAYE

*Y*ou knew all the books but knew not love.

— DAVID DIOP

*T*o love is to make of one's heart a swinging door.

— HOWARD THURMAN

I f we love a child, and the child senses that we love him, he will get a concept of love that all subsequent hatred in the world will never be able to destroy.

— HOWARD THURMAN

L ove stretches your heart and makes you big inside.

— MARGARET WALKER

N o love is innocent. There does not exist a relation between man and woman that does not have its deep, hidden, graying ember of carnality, stubbornly aglow.

— FRANK YERBY

L ove takes off the mask that we fear we cannot live with and know we cannot live without.

— ROBERT SLATER

L ove will open your mind like the chaste leaf in the morning when the sun first touches it.

— WOLE SOYINKA

The Black experience is 360 degrees. Love and sex are probably two of them, but there are 358 more.

—GIL SCOTT-HERON

[M]ost people have a harder time letting themselves love than finding someone to love them.

—BILL RUSSELL

Applause is a kind of love, and when people applaud you, that's love.

—JOE LOUIS

[L]ove is like a virus. It can happen to anybody at any time.

—MAYA ANGELOU

Most of us love from our need to love, not because we find someone deserving.

—NIKKI GIOVANNI

T hin love ain't love at all.

— TONI MORRISON

... *t* he one I trust is the one I love. . . . The one she loves is definitely the one she can trust.

— BILL COSBY

K now that those who hate you are more numerous than those who love you.

— CHANANGA PROVERB

I f men swear to do you harm, spend your night sleeping, but if women swear to do you harm, spend your night awake.

— ETHIOPIAN PROVERB

D ites moi qui vous aimez, et je vous dirai qui vous êtes. (Tell me whom you love, and I'll tell you who you are.)

— LOUISIANA CREOLE PROVERB

*T*he more you began to mean to me, the more I was losing control—and I hated it. I wasn't angry at you for phoning later than you said you would, for ending an evening early because you were genuinely tired—I was angry at myself for allowing it to matter that much.

—GLORIA NAYLOR

*H*ow dumb to be sentimental about anything
To call it love
& cry pathetically
into the long black handkerchief
of the years.

—LEROI JONES (AMIRI BARAKA)

*T*he human heart is a strange mystery.

—ALEXANDRE DUMAS

*M*oney

... **s** ave your money—live economically—dispense with finery, and the gaities [*sic*] which have rendered us proverbial, and save your money.

—AN ADDRESS TO THE COLORED PEOPLE OF THE
UNITED STATES FROM THE COLORED NATIONAL
CONVENTION OF 1848

A ll men cannot go to college but some men must; every isolated group or nation must have its yeast, must have for the talented few centers of training where men are not so mystified and befuddled by the hard and necessary toil of earning a living, as to have no aims higher than their bellies, and no God greater than Gold.

—W. E. B. DU BOIS

[M] oney, it turned out, was exactly like sex, you thought of nothing else if you didn't have it and thought of other things if you did.

— JAMES BALDWIN

L et the Afro-American depend on no party, but on himself, for his salvation. Let him continue toward education, character, and above all, put money in his purse.

— IDA B. WELLS

E verything costs a lot of money when you haven't any.

— JOE LOUIS

M oney is the sun that makes you shine.

— JUNE JORDAN

O nce upon a time freedom used to be life. Now it's money.

— LORRAINE HANSBERRY

*M*oney is the manifestation of power.

—S. E. ANDERSON

*W*here there is money, there is fighting.

—MARIAN ANDERSON

*T*he important thing is not how much money a person makes, it is what he does with it that matters.

—ARTHUR P. GASTON

*A*ll the money in the world will not buy you a kid who will do homework, or maturity for a kid who needs it. It may buy a kid who knows how to buy.

—BILL COSBY

*P*olitics doesn't control the world, money does.

—ANDREW YOUNG

All the money in the world doesn't mean a thing if you don't have time to enjoy it.

— OPRAH WINFREY

When one offers bread to honorable men it is a gift, but to give to any dishonorable men is charity.

— BENIN PROVERB

The bad things I do are the only things that ever make me any money.

— LANGSTON HUGHES

Money is a great dignifier.

— PAUL LAURENCE DUNBAR

Motivation

*E*very blow of the sledge-hammer, wielded by a sable arm, is a powerful blow in support of our cause. Every colored mechanic, is by virtue of circumstances, an elevator of his race. Every house built by black men, is a strong tower against the allied hosts of prejudice.

— AN ADDRESS TO THE COLORED PEOPLE OF THE
UNITED STATES FROM THE COLORED NATIONAL
CONVENTION OF 1848

I was going through the hardest thing, also the greatest thing, for any human being to do; to accept that which is already within you, and around you.

— MALCOLM X

L aughs, kidding and ridicule are often great for a player's motivation, and motivation is the greatest mystery in any champion athlete.

— BILL RUSSELL

T he word "yes" may bring trouble; the word "no" leads nowhere.

— BANTU PROVERB

W hat a man has not is often the only thing that he wants.

— SUDANESE PROVERB

C aution comes from God and haste from the devil.

— BANTU PROVERB

N egroes are Americans and their destiny is the country's destiny. They have no other experience besides their experience on this continent and it is an experience which cannot be rejected, which yet remains to be embraced.

— JAMES BALDWIN

We need the storm, the whirlwind, and the earthquake. The feeling of the nation must be quickened; the conscience of the nation must be aroused; the propriety of the nation must be started; the hypocrisy of the nation must be exposed, and its crimes against God and man denounced.

—FREDERICK DOUGLASS

. . . the upstart of today is the elite of tomorrow.

—SAMUEL RINGGOLD WARD

He had an important and definite object before him, and was willing to sacrifice sleep and rest in order to accomplish it. It was not his own liberty alone, but the freedom of his wife and five children.

—AMANDA BERRY SMITH

Music

F iddlin' nigger say hit's long ways ter de dance.

—FROM A SLAVE NARRATIVE

I f you cannot sing a congregational song at full power, you cannot fight in any struggle. . . . It is something you learn. We would sing together, we would invoke the spirit. We would sing about anything we felt. We would sing about why we sing. We would sing, "The reason I sing this song, Lord, I don't want to be lost." We would sing about the abuses we suffered, like not being allowed to vote. We would sing songs of sorrow and songs of hope.

—DOROTHY COTTON

I n popular music, as in the music of religious fervor, there is a style that is unmistakable, and its origin is certainly no mystery.

—JAMES BALDWIN

*L*et the martial songs be written, let the dirges disappear.

— MARGARET WALKER

. . . *t*here is no true American music but the wild sweet melodies of the Negro slave. . . .

— W. E. B. Du Bois

*T*he music doesn't change governments. Some bureaucrat or some politician isn't going to be changed by some music he hears. But we can change people—individual people. The people can change governments.

— CORDELL REAGON

*T*hey are the music of an unhappy people, of the children of disappointment; they tell of death and suffering and un-voiced longing toward a truer world, of misty wanderings and hidden ways.

— W. E. B. Du Bois

*M*ichael, haul the boat ashore,
Then you'll hear the horn they blow,
Then you'll hear the trumpet sound,
Trumpet sound the world around,
Trumpet sound for rich and poor,
Trumpet sound the Jubilee,
Trumpet sound for you and me.

— TRADITIONAL SONG

*I*t is only in his music, which Americans are able to ad-
mire because a protective sentimentality limits their understanding of it, that the Negro in America has been able to
tell his story.

— JAMES BALDWIN

*L*ift every voice and sing
Till earth and heaven ring,
Ring with the harmonies of Liberty;
Let our rejoicing rise
High as the listening skies,
Let it resound loud as the rolling sea.

— JAMES WELDON JOHNSON

... *I* heard my people singing—in the glow of parlor coalstone and on summer porches sweet with lilac air, from choir loft and Sunday morning pews—and my soul was filled with their harmonies.

—PAUL ROBESON

*M*usic is my mistress, and she plays second fiddle to no one.

—DUKE ELLINGTON

*O*pportunity

*D*on't loaf 'round de corners an' pend on de Lord fuh yo' daily bread. De Lord ain't running no bakery.

—BERT WILLIAMS

*T*he future is, to the young man of color who is in earnest, glorious. Everything is before us; everything to win!

—JONATHAN C. GIBBS

E verybody can be great, because anybody can serve. You don't have to have a college degree to serve. You don't have to make your subject and your verb agree to serve. You don't have to know about Plato and Aristotle to serve. You don't have to know Einstein's Theory of Relativity to serve. You don't have to know the second theory of thermo-dynamics to serve. You only need a heart full of grace. A soul generated by love.

—MARTIN LUTHER KING, JR.

M ore and more . . . an intelligent realization of the great discrepancy between the American social creed and the American social practice forces upon the Negro the taking of the moral advantage that is his.

—ALAIN LOCKE

I f Paul Robeson had not been there, I would not be here. And so it is with the youth of today. The stand you took will help us with a stand in the days, weeks, months, and years ahead, for peace, for the rights and needs of the people.

—SIDNEY POITIER

Poverty

You sift the meal,
You give me the husk.
You cook the bread,
You give me the crust
You fry your meat,
You give me the skin.
And that's where mama's trouble
begin.

— SLAVE SONG DESCRIBING LEFTOVER FOOD

When you're poor, you grow up fast.

— BILLIE HOLIDAY

. . . it's *impossible* to eat enough if you're worried about the next meal.

— JAMES BALDWIN

People who have no children can be hard:
Attain a mail of ice and insolence:
Need not pause in the fire, and in no sense
Hesitate in the hurricane to guard.

. . . .

What shall I give my children? who are poor,
Who are adjudged the leastwise of the land,
Who are my sweetest lepers, who demand
No velvet and no velvety velour . . .

—GWENDOLYN BROOKS

To be a poor man is hard, but to be a poor race in a land
of dollars is the very bottom of hardships.

—W. E. B. DU BOIS

There is something about poverty that smells like death.
Dead dreams dropping off the heart like leaves in dry season
and rotting around the feet; impulses smothered too long in
the fetid air of underground caves. The soul lives in sickly
air.

—ZORA NEALE HURSTON

. . . *i* f there is no future for the black ghetto, the future of all Negroes is diminished. What affects it, affects me, for I am a child of the ghetto.

—STANLEY SANDERS

*P*ower

I t's not about words, it's about spirit.

—CORDELL REAGON

P ower in defense of freedom is greater than power on behalf of tyranny.

—MALCOLM X

T he love of power is one of the greatest human infirmities, and with it comes the usurping influence of despotism, the mother of slavery.

—WILLIAM WHIPPER

Power is the only argument that satisfies man.
— MARCUS GARVEY

[Power] is a whirlwind among breezes.
— ZORA NEALE HURSTON

Power always involves a man in a network of compromise.
— HOWARD THURMAN

We ourselves have the power to end the terror and win for ourselves peace and security. We have the power of numbers, the power of organization, and the power of spirit.
— PAUL ROBESON

This is the only way you end oppression—with power.
— MALCOLM X

There is nothing essentially wrong with power. The problem is American power is unequally distributed.

—MARTIN LUTHER KING, JR.

Power is the ability to achieve purpose.

—MARTIN LUTHER KING, JR.

Do not call for Black power or green power. Call for brain power.

—BARBARA JORDAN

Nobody is as powerful as we make them out to be.

—ALICE WALKER

Strong people don't need strong leaders.

—ELLA J. BAKER

Only the dog's master can take the bone from its mouth.

—SENEGALESE PROVERB

The slave turned inside out quickly becomes the tyrant.

— YORUBA PROVERB

. . . any Black human being able to survive the horrendous and evil circumstances in which one inevitably finds oneself trapped must be some kind of a giant with great and peculiar abilities, with an armor as resistant as steel yet made of purest gold.

— ABBEY LINCOLN

. . . money and property and machines are only projections and sublimations of the power in the body, not power itself.

— PAT ROBINSON AND GROUP

The active influences of the Negro have come out of his strength; his passive influences out of his weaknesses. And it would be well for the nation to remember that for the good of one's own soul, what he needs most to guard against, most to fear, in dealing with another, is that one's weakness, not his strength.

— JAMES WELDON JOHNSON

The power of the ballot we need in sheer self-defense—else what shall save us from a second slavery?

—W. E. B. Du Bois

Pride

De proudness un a man don't count w'en his head's cold.

—FROM A SLAVE NARRATIVE

Anytime you commences to git de big head, you oughter stop an' think 'bout all de grate men whut's died an' 'bout how well de worl' got long widout 'em.

—BERT WILLIAMS

We are not wood, we are not stone, but men, with feelings and sensibilities like other men whose skin is of a lighter hue.

—JOSEPH RAINEY

We at Malcolm X Academy will strive for excellence in our quest to be the best. We will rise above every challenge with our heads held high. We'll always keep the faith when others say die. March on till victory is ours: Amandla!"

— STUDENT OATH

Pappy was a African. I knows dat. He come from Congo, over in Africa, and I heard him say a big storm drove de ship somewhere on de Ca'lina coast. I 'member he mighty 'spectful to Massa and missy, but he proud, too, and walk straighter'n anybody I ever seen. He had scars on de right side he head and cheek what he say am tribe marks, but what dey means I don't know.

— SHACK THOMAS, A FLORIDA SLAVE

Once I redemption neither sought nor knew.

— PHILLIS WHEATLEY

The best blood in my veins is African blood, and I am not ashamed of it.

— FRANCES ELLEN WATKINS HARPER

The civil rights movement that rearranged the social order in this country did not emanate from the halls of the Harvards and the Princetons and Cornells. It came from simple unlettered people who learned that they had the right to stand tall and that nobody can ride a back that isn't bent.

— DOROTHY COTTON

... there is an unconquerable disposition in the breasts of the blacks, which, when it is fully awakened and put in motion, will be subdued, only with the destruction of the animal existence.

— DAVID WALKER

From any point of view, I had rather be what I am, a member of the Negro race, than be able to claim membership with the most favoured of any other race.

— BOOKER T. WASHINGTON

For nobler themes demand a nobler strain,
And purer language on the ethereal plain,

— PHILLIS WHEATLEY

[P]ride . . . If you haven't got it, you can't show it. If you have got it, you can't hide it.

—ZORA NEALE HURSTON

Black is beautiful.

—ANONYMOUS

When the Negro learns what manner of man he is spiritually, he will wake up all over. . . . He will rise in the majesty of his own soul. He will glorify the beauty of his own brown skin . . . and he will redeem his body and rescue his soul. . . .

—NANNIE BURROUGHS

We never signed a pact either on paper or in our hearts to turn the other cheek forever and ever when we were assaulted.

—ROY WILKINS

We have no reason to complain until we take pride in our own.

—C. H. J. TAYLOR

One of the most promising of young Negro poets said to me once, "I want to be a poet—not a Negro poet," meaning, I believe, "I want to write like a white poet"; meaning subconsciously, "I would like to be a white poet"; meaning behind that, "I would like to be white." And I was sorry the young man said that, for no great poet has ever been afraid of being himself.

—LANGSTON HUGHES

Say it loud, I'm black and I'm proud.

—JAMES BROWN

Say, Comrade, here's the wild river that's got to be harnessed and directed. Here's that *something,* that pent-up folk consciousness. Here's a fleeting glimpse of the heart of the Negro, the heart that beats and suffers and hopes—for freedom. Here's that fluid something that's like iron. Here's the real dynamite that Joe Louis uncovered!

—NEW MASSES, OCTOBER 8, 1935

*S*on, after I'm gone I want you to keep up the good fight. I never told you, but our life is a war and I have been a traitor all my born days, a spy in the enemy's country ever since I give up my gun back in the Reconstruction. Live with your head in the lion's mouth. I want you to overcome 'em with yeses, undermine 'em with grins, agree 'em to death and destruction, let 'em swoller you till they vomit or bust wide open.

— RALPH ELLISON

*T*here is enough history to make one proud of his race. Why not then teach the child more of himself and less of others, more of his elevation and less of his degradation? This can produce true pride of race, which begets mutual confidence and unity.

— D. A. STRAKER

*T*each the children pride. Nothing learned is worth anything if you don't know how to be proud of yourself.

— NANNIE BURROUGHS

*T*he hole in a poor man's garment is soon filled with the patchwork of pride. . . .

— WOLE SOYINKA

I f our people are to fight their way out of bondage we must arm them with the sword and the shield and the buckler or pride—belief in themselves and their possibilities based on a sure knowledge of the past.

—MARY MCLEOD BETHUNE

W e used to be "shiftless and lazy," now we are "fearsome and awesome." I think the Black man should take pride in that.

—JAMES EARL JONES

N ever let pride be your guiding principle. Let your accomplishments speak for you.

—MORGAN FREEMAN

W e are the Blackest and the bravest race.

—FROM A LETTER BY A BLACK MAN TO ABRAHAM LINCOLN, 1863

Black pride, young black pride
Like Moses, you will lead our people over
And through.

— MARGARET GOSS BURROUGHS

The fact that white people readily and proudly call themselves "white," glorify all that is white, and whitewash all
that is glorified, becomes unnatural and bigoted in its intent
only when these same whites deny persons of African heritage who are Black the natural and inalienable right to
readily and proudly call themselves "black," glorify all that
is black, and blackwash all that is glorified.

— ABBEY LINCOLN

... to attain his place in the world, he must be himself
and not another.

— W. E. B. DU BOIS

Let others bare their backs to the lash, and meekly and
submissively wear their chains.

— ROBERT PURVIS

The New Negro,
Hard-muscled, Fascist-hating, Democracy-ensouled,
Strides in seven-league boots
Along the Highway of Today
Toward the Promised Land of Tomorrow!

— MELVIN B. TOLSON

To fling my arms wide
In the face of the sun,
Dance! Whirl! Whirl!
Till the quick day is done.
Rest at pale evening . . .
A tall, slim tree . . .
Night coming tenderly
Black like me.

— LANGSTON HUGHES

We wish our race pride to be a healthier, more positive achievement than a feeling based upon a realization of the shortcomings of others.

— ALAIN LOCKE

I will not retreat one thousandth of an inch.

—PAUL ROBESON

I f the majority rules, then the earth belongs to colored people.

—CHARLES VICTOR ROMAN

L ift up yourselves . . . take yourselves out of the mire and hitch your hopes to the stars.

—MARCUS GARVEY

Racism

I f you're white, you're right,
If you're brown, stick around,
If you're black, get back.

—ANONYMOUS

I had a hard lesson to learn, that I could not help others free their hearts and minds of racial prejudice unless I would do all I could within myself to straighten out my own thinking and to feel and respond to kindness, to goodwill from wherever it came, whether it was the southerner, northerner, or any race.

—ROSA PARKS

*I*n the context of the Negro problem neither whites nor blacks, for excellent reasons of their own, have the faintest desire to look back; but I think that the past is all that makes the present coherent, and further, that the past will remain horrible for exactly as long as we refuse to assess it honestly.

—JAMES BALDWIN

*T*his is not a Democratic Government if a numerous, law-abiding, industrious, and useful class of citizens, born and bred on the soil, are to be treated as aliens and enemies, as an inferior degraded class, who must have no voice in the Government which they support, protect and defend with all their heart, soul, mind, and body, both in peace and war.

—FROM A PETITION TO THE TENNESSEE
CONSTITUTIONAL CONVENTION TO GRANT
AFRICAN AMERICANS THE RIGHT TO VOTE

I am conscious of the fact that mere connection with what is known as a superior race will not permanently carry an individual forward unless he has individual worth, and mere connection with what is regarded as an inferior race will not finally hold an individual back if he possesses intrinsic, individual merit.

—BOOKER T. WASHINGTON

T he real solution of the race problem lies in the children, both so far as we who are oppressed and those who oppress us are concerned.

—MARY CHURCH TERRELL

B eing black in America has nothing to do with skin color. To be black means that your soul, your mind and your body are where the dispossessed are.

—JAMES CONE

A nything that is as old as racism is in the blood line of the nation. It's not any superficial thing—that attitude is in the blood and we have to educate it out.

—NANNIE BURROUGHS

[A] ny Negro, if he were honest, would have to say that in our democracy at present, that he is never, for any one second, unconscious of the fact that he is a black American. He can never be unconscious of it in any part of the United States.

—PAUL ROBESON

I t was awful to be Negro and have no control over my life. It was brutal to be young and already trained to sit quietly and listen to charges brought against my color with no chance of defense. We should all be dead. I thought I should like to see us all dead, one on top of the other.

—MAYA ANGELOU

R acism shows the bankruptcy of man.

—FRANTZ FANON

S ince the earliest days of this nation's history, students attending its schools have achieved competence in the four, not three, "Rs," Reading, Riting, Rithmetic, and Racism.

—MALCOLM X

. . . *r* acism is a sickness unto death.

—MARTIN LUTHER KING, JR.

I hate racism and I'm out to smash it or it's going to smash me.

—STOKELY CARMICHAEL

R acism is so universal in this country, so widespread and deep-seated, that it is invisible because it is so normal.

—SHIRLEY CHISHOLM

R acism is a scholarly pursuit, it's taught, it's institutionalized.

—TONI MORRISON

R acism seems ageless—like the passion of those who war against it.

—GORDON PARKS

*R*acism is not an excuse to not do the best you can.

— ARTHUR ASHE

*A*nd happy is that nation which makes the Bible its rule of action, and obeys principle, not prejudice.

— FROM A PETITION TO THE TENNESSEE
CONSTITUTIONAL CONVENTION TO GRANT
AFRICAN AMERICANS THE RIGHT TO VOTE

"*M*y boss is white," said Simple.
"Most bosses are," I said.

— LANGSTON HUGHES

*S*egregation, the monster that had terrorized my parents and driven them out of the green Eden in which they had been born, was itself vulnerable and could be attacked, possibly destroyed. I felt as if I had witnessed the first act of a spectacular drama. I wanted to stay around for the second.

— ARNA BONTEMPS

... *n*o matter how liberal, how well accepted into the white community, no matter how popular or famous, no matter how unprejudiced a Negro may be, most of us have to wear some sort of mask outside our own group, and it's a relief to be able to put that mask down from time to time when we're back with our own kind.

—ALTHEA GIBSON

Respect

*S*terner necessities will bring higher respect.
—AN ADDRESS TO THE COLORED PEOPLE OF THE
UNITED STATES FROM THE COLORED NATIONAL
CONVENTION OF 1848

*T*reat the world well. . . . It was not given to you by your parents. . . . It was lent to you by your children.

—KENYAN PROVERB

*L*et no man of us budge one step, and let slaveholders come to beat us from our country. America is more our country, than it is the whites'—we have enriched it with our *blood and tears*. The greatest riches in all America have arisen from our blood and tears.

— DAVID WALKER

*[N]*either the old-time slavery, nor continued prejudice need extinguish self-respect, crush manly ambition or paralyze effort.

— PAUL ROBESON

A race without authority and power is a race without respect.

— MARCUS GARVEY

*R*espect me or put me to death.

— MALCOLM X

Do not confuse respect with knowledge. Remember, before one has white hairs, one must first have them black.

— OUSMANE SEMBENE

We are not fighting for the right to be like you. We respect ourselves too much for that.

— JOHN OLIVER KILLENS

What the Western world has done is believe that the people it has conquered are inferior to it and different from it. This is a deceit no one could have held for long without great effect on their reason.

— JAMES BALDWIN

That cop was powerful mean.
First he called me, "Black boy."
Then he punched me in the face
and drug me by the collar to a wall
and made me lean against it with my hands spread
while he searched me,
and all the time he searched me
he kicked me and cuffed me and cussed me.

I was mad enough
to lay him out,
and would've did it, only
I didn't want to hurt his feelings,
and lose the good will

of the good white folks downtown,
who hired him.

—DUDLEY RANDALL

... *h*uman beings cannot be willed and molded into non-
existence.

—ANGELA YVONNE DAVIS

*R*esponsibility

*H*eap o' people rickerlec' favors by markin' 'em down in
the snow.

—FROM A SLAVE NARRATIVE

f ellow citizens, rights impose duties. We are not now, as once we were, without responsibility because without power, without duties because without rights. Are we so ignorant as to imagine that the world will not hold us to account for our use of these rights?

—ROBERT B. ELLIOTT

I cannot walk upon your legs, or you upon mine. I cannot breathe for you, or you for me; I must breathe for myself, and you for yourself.

—FREDERICK DOUGLASS

A nd while we are demanding and ought to demand . . . God forbid that we should ever forget to urge corresponding duties upon our people:

The duty to vote.
The duty to respect the rights of others.
The duty to work.
The duty to obey the laws.
The duty to be clean and orderly.
The duty to send our children to school.
The duty to respect ourselves, even as we respect others.

—THE NIAGARA MOVEMENT

... *a* sense of responsibility which comes with power is the rarest of things.

—ALEXANDER CRUMMELL

... *o* ne must never, in one's own life, accept these injustices as commonplace but must fight them with all one's strength.

—JAMES BALDWIN

... *e* very person has a name, a place, and the responsibility for which no other can answer.

—OTIS MOSS

B e responsible for our actions, and take responsible actions.

—HAKI MADHUBUTI

Black Americans must begin to accept a larger share of responsibility for their lives. . . . I don't believe that we will produce strong soldiers by moaning about what the enemy has done to us.

—JESSE JACKSON

A knife does not know its master.

—NNOBI PROVERB

This is a democracy—a government of the people. It should aim to make every man, without regard to the color of his skin, the amount of his wealth, or the character of his religious faith, feel personally interested in its welfare.

—FROM A PETITION TO THE TENNESSEE CONSTITUTIONAL CONVENTION TO GRANT AFRICAN AMERICANS THE RIGHT TO VOTE

Responsibility is one of those ten-dollar words tossed around us as lightly as love and free sex. Think about that— free sex! Nothing is free these days and certainly not sex.

—NIKKI GIOVANNI

*T*here is only one thing to save the Negro, and that is an immediate realization of his own responsibilities.

—MARCUS GARVEY

*R*evolution

*I*t's time to bring down the volume and bring up the program.

—AL SHARPTON

*F*or years now I have heard the word "Wait!" It rings in the ear of every Negro with piercing familiarity. This "Wait" has almost always meant "Never." . . .

—MARTIN LUTHER KING, JR.

*D*oes the Lord condescend to hear their cries and see their tears in consequence of oppression? Will he let the oppressors rest comfortably and happy always? Will he not cause the very children of the oppressors to rise up against them and ofttimes put them to death?

— DAVID WALKER

*A*ction! not criticism, [was] the plain duty of this hour.

— FREDERICK DOUGLASS

*W*ho would be free themselves must strike the blow.

— FREDERICK DOUGLASS

I don't accept the world the way it works. I take on the world. I want to make the world the way it should be.

— BERNICE JOHNSON REAGON

*W*e never lost hope despite the segregated world of this rural town because we had adults who gave us a sense of a future—and black folk had an extra lot of problems, and we were taught that we could struggle and change them.

— MARIAN WRIGHT EDELMAN

There was only one thing I could do—hammer relentlessly, continually crying aloud, even if in a wilderness, and force open, by sheer muscle power, every closed door.

—ADAM CLAYTON POWELL, JR.

Power concedes nothing without a demand. It never did and it never will.

—FREDERICK DOUGLASS

Things will happen and things will change. The only thing that's really worth-while is change. It's coming.

—SEPTIMA CLARK

One thing they cannot prohibit—
The strong men . . . coming on
The strong men gittin' stronger.
Strong men . . .
Stronger . . .

—STERLING A. BROWN

*M*en must not only know, they must act.

—W. E. B. Du Bois

*W*e are gathered here in the largest demonstration in the history of this nation. Let the nation and the world know the meaning of our numbers. We are not pressure groups, we are not an organization or a group of organizations, we are not a mob. We are the advance guard of a massive moral revolution for jobs and freedom.

—A. Philip Randolph

*T*he hour is late; the clock of destiny is ticking out.

—Martin Luther King, Jr.

*A*gitators are inevitable. They are as necessary to social organism as blood is to animal organism. Revolution follows as matter of course.

—T. Thomas Fortune

*N*ot until [the] revolution of mind is completed will there be a fair chance for the full development of those principles of brotherhood and liberty which we hold as ideals.

—MARY McLEOD BETHUNE

*P*eace and revolution make uneasy bedfellows.

—ALBERT LUTHULI

*R*evolution is like a forest fire, it burns everything in its path.

—MALCOLM X

*T*here is no violent revolution except as a result of the Black mind expanding, trying to take control of its own space.

—LEROI JONES (AMIRI BARAKA)

*R*evolutionaries are not necessarily born poor or in the ghetto.

—H. RAP BROWN

*A*nyone who thinks that he can stop a natural revolution by means of repression should muster all the National Guardsmen that he can find, tell them to cross a pregnant woman's legs and see if they can stop the baby from being born.

— DICK GREGORY

*W*e have tomorrow
Bright before us
Like a flame.

Yesterday, a night-gone thing
A sun-down name.

And dawn today
Broad arch above the road we came.
We march!

— CITED BY ALAIN LOCKE

I am not tragically colored. There is no great sorrow dammed up in my soul nor lurking behind my eyes. . . . I do not belong to the sobbing school of Negrohood who hold that nature somehow has given them a lowdown dirty deal and whose feelings are hurt about it. . . . No, I do not weep at the world—I am too busy sharpening my oyster knife.

— ZORA NEALE HURSTON

I n any nonviolent campaign there are four basic steps: (1) collection of the facts to determine whether injustices are alive, (2) negotiation, (3) self-purification, and (4) direct action.

—MARTIN LUTHER KING, JR.

C haos occurs when human rights are not respected.

—ANDREW YOUNG

O ne does not glorify in romanticizing revolution. One cries.

—LORRAINE HANSBERRY

R evolution arises out of need. Revolution is we need to change our ways of being with one another. Revolution is we need one another.

—AL YOUNG

We are unfair, and unfair.
We are black magicians, black arts
we make in black labs of the heart.
The fair are
fair and death
ly white.

The day will not save them
and we own
the night.

—LeRoi Jones (Amiri Baraka)

Revolution begins with the self, in the self.

—Toni Cade Bambara

Mapping out a building takeover when your term paper is overdue and your scholarship is under review is not revolutionary.

—Toni Cade Bambara

I , the Negro, like my counterparts in Asia and Africa and South America and on the islands of the many seas, am refusing to be your "nigger" any longer. Even some of us "favored," "talented," "unusual," ones are refusing to be your educated, sophisticated, split-leveled "niggers" any more. We refuse to look at ourselves through the eyes of white America.

—JOHN OLIVER KILLENS

Out of the dead-ends of Poverty,
Through wildernesses of Superstition,
Across barricades of Jim Crowism . . .
We advance!

With the Peoples of the World . . .
We advance!

—MELVIN B. TOLSON

. . . Carry hate
In front of you and harmony behind.
Be deaf to music and to beauty blind.
Win war. Rise bloody, maybe not too late
For having first to civilize a space
Wherein to play your violin with grace.

—GWENDOLYN BROOKS

*L*et us come together by the thousands from all parts of this slaveholding nation and . . . kindle up the sacred fires of liberty upon the altars of our hearts, which shall never be extinguished until the last slave of America is free.

— HENRY BIBB

*L*et your motto be resistance, resistance, RESISTANCE! No oppressed people have ever secured their liberty without resistance.

— HENRY HIGHLAND GARNET

*P*eace is the exhaustion of strife, and is only secure in her triumphs in being in instant readiness for war. . . .

— MIFFLIN WISTAR GIBBS

*W*hite folks don't want peace; they want quiet. The price you pay for peace is justice. Until there is justice, there will be no peace or quiet.

— JESSE JACKSON

Shame

Our vices and our degradation are ever arrayed against us, but our virtues are passed by unnoticed.

—EDITORIAL FROM THE FIRST EDITION OF
FREEDOM'S JOURNAL

... my Jim Crow education assumed quite a different form. It was no longer brutally cruel, but subtly cruel. Here I learned to lie, to steal, to dissemble. I learned to play that dual role which every Negro must play if he wants to eat and live.

—RICHARD WRIGHT

Crime has no sex and yet today
    I wear the brand of shame;
Whilst he amid the gay and proud
    Still bears an honored name.

—FRANCIS ELLEN WATKINS HARPER

A woman who could bend to grief
But would not bend to shame.
— FRANCIS ELLEN WATKINS HARPER

T here was no one more forbearing than Aunt Jemima, no one stronger or more pious or more loyal or more wise; there was, at the same time, no one weaker or more faithless or more vicious and certainly no one more immoral.
— JAMES BALDWIN

Signifying

Y ou fool, you thirty cents away from having a quarter. You raggedy as a roach, eat the hole out a donut . . . Look at you! Shoes so run over, you got to lay down to put 'em on.
— SPIKE LEE

You so black till they have to throw a sheet over yo' head so de sun kin rise every mornin'.

— ZORA NEALE HURSTON

A: Jim, you so ugly you got to sneak up on the dark.
B: You so dark you ain' seen daylight in ten years.
C: You the only dude I know can cast a shadow on coal.

— ANONYMOUS

Man, why don't you put that broom down, you know you don't know nothin' 'bout no machinery.

— ANONYMOUS

When she sat down to get a haircut she opened her shirt.

— ANONYMOUS

His momma so bald, when she go to sleep at night her head keep slippin' off the pillow.

— WILL SMITH

You're sharp as a 'skeeter's peter and that's sharp at both ends.

— STREET SAYING

The kettle callin' the pot black, an' the fryin' pan standin' up for witness.

— STREET SAYING

Your mama is like a doorknob. Everybody gets a turn.

— STREET SAYING

Your mother thinks she's a big wheel because her face looks like a hubcap.

— STREET SAYING

Your mama is so fat, she could sell shade.

— STREET SAYING

She's so fat, when she was missing, they had to put her picture on a milk truck.

— STREET SAYING

Your father is so stupid, he lost his job as an elevator operator because he forgot the route.

— STREET SAYING

She's so ugly, she goes to the beauty parlor in an ambulance.

— STREET SAYING

Your butt is so big, when you back up, you beep.

— STREET SAYING

Your mama smells so bad, bloodhounds won't chase her.

— STREET SAYING

Your house is so dirty, the roaches have to wear shoes.

— STREET SAYING

Your mother so old, she bleeds dust.

— STREET SAYING

Your mother is so greasy, she sweats Crisco.

— STREET SAYING

Your family is so black, if they held hands, they'd look like a stretch limo.

— STREET SAYING

He so white, he thinks Malcolm X means Malcolm the Tenth.

— STREET SAYING

Your mama so black, when she goes out in daylight, the streetlights come on.

— STREET SAYING

. . . s ince she didn't have but one tooth in her whole head they called her Doughnut Puncher.

—DIANE OLIVER

A h seen a man so ugly till they spread a sheet over his head at night so sleep could slip up on him.

—ZORA NEALE HURSTON

Slavery

T he remark is not infrequently made, that slaves are the most contented and happy laborers in the world. They dance and sing, and make all manners of joyful noises—so they do: but it is a great mistake to suppose them happy because they sing. The songs of the slave represent the sorrows, rather than the joys, of his heart. . . .

—FREDERICK DOUGLASS

*M*issus in the big house, Mammy in the yard,
Missus holdin' her white hands, Mammy workin' hard.
I went to Atlanta, Never been dere a fo'.
White folks eat de apple, Nigger wait fo' de co'.
I went to Charleston, Never been dere a fo'.
White folks sleep on feather bed, Nigger on de flo'.

—FROM A SLAVE SONG

*T*he big bee flies high,
The little bee makes the honey;
The black folks makes the cotton,
And the white folks gets the money.

—WILLIAM WELLS BROWN

*O*h, could slavery exist long if it did not sit on a commercial throne?

—FRANCES ELLEN WATKINS HARPER

*S*lavery is gone . . . but the spirit of it still remains.

—FRANCIS JAMES GRIMKÉ

*D*uring the slave *regime,* the Southern white man owned the Negro body and soul. It was to his interest to dwarf the soul and preserve the body.

—W. E. B. Du Bois

. . . *s* lavery is a breeding bed, a sort of composte heap where the best qualities of both races decay and become food for the worst.

—Archibald Henry Grimké

I ask no monument, proud and high,
To arrest the gaze of the passers by;
All that my yearning spirit craves
Is—Bury me not in a land of slaves!

—Frances Ellen Watkins Harper

. . . *m* illions have come from eternity into time, and have returned again to the world of spirits, cursed and ruined by American slavery.

—Henry Highland Garnet

You will see how a man was made a slave, and how a slave was made a man.

— FREDERICK DOUGLASS

The slave trade debauches men's minds, and hardens them to every feeling of humanity.

— OLAUDAH EQUIANO

The singing of a man cast away upon a desolate island might be as appropriately considered as evidence of contentment and happiness, as the singing of a slave; the songs of the one and of the other are prompted by the same emotions.

— FREDERICK DOUGLASS

But slavery attempts to make a man a brute. It treats him as a beast. Its terrible work is not finished until the ruined victim of its lusts, and pride, and avarice, and hatred, is reduced so low that with tearful eyes and feeble voice he faintly cries, *"I am happy and contented—I love this condition."*

— HENRY HIGHLAND GARNET

And before I'd be a slave,
I'd be buried in my grave,
And go home to my Lord and be free.

—CIVIL RIGHTS SONG

We are beautiful people
with african imaginations
full of masks and dances and swelling chants
with african eyes, and noses, and arms,
though we sprawl in grey chains in a place
full of winters, when what we want is sun.

—LEROI JONES (AMIRI BARAKA)

It seems almost incredible that the advocates of liberty should conceive of the idea of selling a fellow creature to slavery.

—JAMES FORTEN

Must I dwell in slavery's night
And all pleasure take its flight
Far beyond my feeble sight,
Forever?

—GEORGE MOSES HORTON

I am opposed to slavery, not because it enslaves the Black man, but because it enslaves man.

— DANIEL PAYNE

I want its root and branch destroyed.

— SOJOURNER TRUTH

*W*hen will all races and classes of men learn that men made in the image of God will not be the slave of another image?

— SUTTON E. GRIGGS

*H*ere was a way to produce a perfect slave. Accustom him to rigid discipline, demand from him unconditional submission, impress upon him a sense of innate inferiority, develop in him a paralyzing fear of white people, train him to adopt the master's code of good behavior, and instill in him a sense of complete dependence.

— MARTIN LUTHER KING, JR.

*A*s long as man is slave to another power, he is not free to serve God with mature responsibility. He is not free to become what he is, human.

—JAMES CONE

*E*very people, every race, has passed through a stage of slavery.

—C. L. R. JAMES

I've been in slavery all my life. Ain't nothing changed for me but the address.

—JAMES BROWN

*I*f you have not liked my grammar, recollect that I was born and brought up under an institution where, if an individual was found teaching me, he would have been sent to the State's prison.

—WILLIAM WELLS BROWN

... *l*et them toil with him in the field—sleep with him in the cabin—feed with him on husks; let them behold him scourged, hunted, trampled on, and they will come back with another story in their mouths. Let them know the heart of the poor slave—learn his secret thoughts—thoughts he dare not utter in the hearing of the white man; let them sit by him in the silent watches of the night—converse with him in trustful confidence, of "life, liberty, and the pursuit of happiness," and they will find that ninety-nine out of every hundred are intelligent enough to understand their situation, and to cherish in their bosoms the love of freedom, as passionately as themselves.

—SOLOMON NORTHUP, TWELVE YEARS A SLAVE

I have often seen slaves, particularly those who were meagre, in different islands, put into scales and weighed, and then sold from three pence to six pence or nine pence a pound. My master, however, whose humanity was shocked at this mode, used to sell such by the lump.

— OLAUDAH EQUIANO

... *t* he facts of American history have in the last half century been falsified because the nation was ashamed. The South was ashamed because it fought to perpetuate human slavery. The North was ashamed because it had to call in the Black men to save the Union, abolish slavery and establish democracy.

—W. E. B. DU BOIS

O Negro slaves, dark purple ripened plums,
Squeezed, and bursting in the pine-wood air,
Passing, before they stripped the old tree bare
One plum was saved for me, one seed becomes

An everlasting song, a singing tree,
Caroling softly souls of slavery,
What they were, and what they are to me,
Caroling softly souls of slavery.

—JEAN TOOMER

The South

Y ou go down there lookin' for justice, that's what you find,
just us!

—RICHARD PRYOR

It is the custom of Democratic journals to stigmatize the Negroes of the South as being in a semi-barbarous condition. Pray tell me, who is the barbarian here, the murderer or his victim?

—ROBERT B. ELLIOTT [IN *CONGRESSIONAL GLOBE*, 42ND CONGRESS, 1ST SESSION]

... my feelings had already been formed by the south, for there had been slowly instilled into my personality and consciousness, Black though I was, the culture of the South.

—RICHARD WRIGHT

South means "south" of the Canadian border.

—MALCOLM X

How big does a person have to grow down in this part of the country before he's going to stand up and say, "Let us stop treating other men and women and children with such cruelty just because they are born colored?"

—MAHALIA JACKSON

*I*f one could discount the sadness, the misery, the near-volcanic intensity of Negro life in most of the South, and concentrate on the mild, almost tropical climate and the beauty of the landscape, one is often tempted to forget the senseless cruelty and inhumanity the strong too often inflict on the weak.

— AARON DOUGLAS

*N*egroes then were stronger than they are now, especially Georgia Negroes. Negroes born in Georgia had to be strong simply to survive.

— MALCOLM X

. . . *W*hy am I compelled
To tread again where buried feet have trod,
To shed my tears where blood and tears have flowed?
. . . Cripples and monsters
Are here. My flesh must make them whole and hale.
I am the sacrifice.

— DUDLEY RANDALL

This was a southern auction, at which the bones, muscles, sinews, blood and nerves of a young lady of sixteen were sold for five-hundred dollars; her moral character for two-hundred; her improved intellect for one-hundred; her Christianity for four-hundred; and her chastity and virtue for three-hundred dollars more. And this, too, in a city thronged with churches, whose tall spires look like so many signals pointing to heaven and whose ministers preach that slavery is a God-ordained institution.

— WILLIAM WELLS BROWN

Success

I have learned that success is to be measured not so much by the position that one has reached in life as by the obstacles which he has overcome while trying to succeed.

— BOOKER T. WASHINGTON

*I*f you can somehow think and dream of success in small steps, every time you make a step, every time you accomplish a small goal, it gives you confidence to go on from there.

— JOHN H. JOHNSON

*T*he individual who can do something that the world wants done will, in the end, make his way regardless of his race.

— BOOKER T. WASHINGTON

*N*othing succeeds like success.

— ALEXANDRE DUMAS

*I*t is better for us to succeed, though some die, than for us to fail though all live.

— WILLIAM PICKENS

*T*here is no force like success, and that is why the individual makes all effort to surround himself throughout life with the evidence of it; as of the individual, so should it be of the nation.

— MARCUS GARVEY

*A*nytime you see someone more successful than you are, they are doing something that you aren't.

— MALCOLM X

*F*amily life is our strength and success.

— JOSEPH LOWERY

*T*o succeed, one must be creative and persistent.

— JOHN H. JOHNSON

*S*uccess is the result of perfection, hard work, learning from failure, loyalty, and persistence.

— COLIN POWELL

One has to have an individual life fulfillment and self-image to succeed as a human being.

— TESS ONWUEME

Success has a power of its own.

— CORDISS COLLINS

If you set out to be successful, then you already are.

— KATHERINE DUNHAM

Success has nothing to do with money . . . it is having an education and nobody being able to take it from you.

— DREW BROWN

Today always comes before tomorrow.

— BOTSWANI PROVERB

*T*here are three things that a man must know to survive long in the world: what is too much for him, what is too little for him, and what is just right for him.

— MALAWI PROVERB

*A*sk of him who has been satisfied and is now hungry; don't ask of him who has been hungry and is now satisfied.

— PYGMY PROVERB

... *y*ou find your Self in destroying illusions, smashing myths, laundering the head of whitewash, being responsible to some truth, to the struggle.

— TONI CADE BAMBARA

*T*he new racial poetry of the Negro is the expression of something more than experimentation in a new technique. It marks the birth of a new racial consciousness and self-conception ... It lacks apology, the wearying appeals to pity, and the conscious philosophy of defense. In being itself it reveals its greatest charm; and in accepting its distinctive life, invests it with a new meaning.

— CHARLES S. JOHNSON

Suffering

Who knows but there may be such a thing as a refined mob, composed of "colonels," "Southern aristocracy" and the ever present "best citizens"? Who knows, after seeing their work, that they have improved on the art of torture practised in savage life and made it more fiendish?

—ROBERT S. ABBOTT

And mothers stood with streaming eyes,
And saw their dearest children sold. . . .

—FRANCES ELLEN WATKINS HARPER

The owl in sadness seeks the caves of night.

—PHILLIS WHEATLEY

*A*h! How lonely suffering is!

— MARIE CHAUVET

*A*nd when this transient life shall end,
Oh, may some kind, eternal friend,
Bid me from servitude ascend,
   Forever!

— GEORGE MOSES HORTON

I KNOW WHAT THE CAGED BIRD FEELS
I know what the caged bird feels, alas!
   When the sun is bright on the upland slopes,
When the wind stirs soft through the springing grass,
And the river flows like a stream of glass;
   When the first bird sings and the first bud opes,
And the faint perfume from its chalice steals—
I know what the caged bird feels!

— PAUL LAURENCE DUNBAR

Why must we remember? Is this but a counsel of Vengeance and Hate? God Forbid! We must remember because if once the world forgets evil, evil is reborn; because if the suffering of the American Negro is once forgotten, then there is no guerdon, down to the last pulse of time, that Devils will not again enslave and maim and murder and oppress the weak and unfortunate.

—CRISIS, AUGUST 1919

Oh, Black known and unknown poets, how often have your auctioned pains sustained us? Who will compute the lonely nights made less lonely by your songs, or by the empty pots made less tragic by your tales?

—MAYA ANGELOU

To know the essence of suffering is to know the essence of joy.

—ALFRED PASTER

Suffering stalks man, never losing the scent, and sooner or later seizes upon him to wreak devastation.

—HOWARD THURMAN

I t is important to be sympathetic to the suffering of people because no people will indefinitely tolerate repression.

—RANDALL ROBINSON

H unger and suffering have no voices of their own.

—KANEM PROVERB

S orrow is like a cloud; when it becomes too heavy it falls.

—ETHIOPIAN PROVERB

W E WEAR THE MASK

We wear the mask that grins and lies,
It hides our cheeks and shades our eyes,
This debt we pay to human guile;
With torn and bleeding hearts we smile,
And mouth with myriad subtleties.

—PAUL LAURENCE DUNBAR

A ll these furnaces of trial as they are, purify and ennoble the man who has to pass through them.

—SAMUEL RINGGOLD WARD

. . . *t* he State of Kentuckey Has contributed of her colored Sons over thirty thousand Soldiers who have illustrated their courage and devotion on Many battle fields and Have Poured out their blood Lavishly in defence of their Country and their Country's flag and we confidently hope this Blood will be carried to our credit in any Political Settlement of our Native State—yet if the government Should give up the State to the control of her civil authorities there is not one of these Soldiers who will Not Suffer all the grinding oppression of her most inhuman laws if not in their own persons yet in the persons of their wives their children and their mothers— . . .

CHA A ROSBOROUGH   JERRE MENINETTEE   R M JOHNSON
HENRY H. WHITE   THOMAS JAMES   WM F. BUTLER

—FROM A LETTER TO PRESIDENT
ANDREW JOHNSON, JUNE 1865

Mexico Mo Dec 30th 1863

M y Dear Husband   I have received your last kind letter a few days ago and was much pleased to hear from you once more. It seems like a long time since you left me. I have had nothing but trouble since you left. You recollect what I told you how they would do after you was gone. they abuse me because you went & say they will not take care of our children & do nothing but quarrel with me all the time and beat me scandalously the day before yesterday— . . . Remember all I told you about how they would do me after you left— for they do worse than they ever did & I do not know what will become of me & my poor little children. Oh I wish you had staid with me & not gone till I could go with you for I do nothing but grieve all the time about you. write & tell me when you are coming.

— MARTHA GLOVER, WIFE OF AN
AFRICAN-AMERICAN UNION SOLDIER

I 'm rolling through an unfriendly worl'.

— TRADITIONAL SPIRITUAL

S ometimes I feel like a motherless child,
A long way from home. . . .

— TRADITIONAL SPIRITUAL

T rouble—trouble has followed me all my days,
Trouble—trouble has followed me all my days—
Seems like trouble's gonna follow me always.

— TRADITIONAL BLUES

*I*n my time, I have been cut, stabbed, run over, hit by a car, tromped by a horse, robbed, fooled, deceived, double-crossed, dealt seconds, and might near blackmailed—but I am still here! I have been laid off, fired and not rehired, Jim Crowed, segregated, insulted, eliminated, locked in, locked out, locked up, left holding the bag, and denied relief. I have been caught in the rain, caught in jails, caught short with my rent, and caught with the wrong woman—but I am still here! . . . I have been underfed, underpaid, undernourished, and everything but undertaken—yet I am still here."

—LANGSTON HUGHES

I walk through the churchyard
   To lay this body down;
I know moon-rise, I know star-rise;
I walk in the moonlight, I walk in the starlight;
I'll lie in the grave and stretch out my arms,
I'll go to judgment in the evening of the day,
And my soul and thy soul shall meet that day,
   When I lay this body down.

—TRADITIONAL SONG

*T*his is the red man's country by natural right, and the black man's by virtue of his suffering and toil.

—ROBERT PURVIS

*A*las! The journey of life is beset with thorns to those who have to pursue it alone.

—ALEXANDRE DUMAS

Truth

*A*rt is the ability to tell the truth, especially about oneself.

—RICHARD PRYOR

*T*here is a feminine as well as a masculine side to truth; that these are related not as inferior and superior, not as better and worse, not as weaker and stronger, but as complements—complements in one necessary and symmetric whole.

—ANNA J. COOPER

A man is his words.

— AFRICAN PROVERB

E verything I tell you is the truth, but there's plenty I can't tell you.

— SLAVE

A nd if thou boast TRUTH to utter,
SPEAK, and leave the rest to God.

— MARTIN DELANY

I have great faith in the power and influence of facts. It is seldom that anything is permanently gained by holding back a fact.

— BOOKER T. WASHINGTON

I f you raise up truth, it's magnetic. It has a way of drawing people.

— JESSE JACKSON

*T*hreats cannot supress the truth.

— IDA B. WELLS

I swore to myself that if I ever wrote another book, no one would weep over it; that it would be so hard and deep that they would have to face it without the consolation of tears.

— RICHARD WRIGHT

*T*ruth comes down to us from the past, then, like gold washed down from the mountains.

— CARTER G. WOODSON

*T*ruth burns up error.

— SOJOURNER TRUTH

I'm for truth, no matter who tells it.

— MALCOLM X

[T]ruth pressed to earth will rise again.

—MARTIN LUTHER KING, JR.

Who loves Truth loves God, for God is Truth.

—FRANK YERBY

Truth alone is powerless against power, but truth fused with power is more powerful than power alone.

—LERONE BENNETT, JR.

Truth is that which places a man in touch with the real; once found, he is prepared to give all for it.

—JAMES CONE

Truth is the baby of the world, it never gets old.

—DICK GREGORY

The eyes believe themselves; the ears believe others; and the heart believes the truth.

—IBO PROVERB

Words spoken at night are coated with butter; as soon as the sun shines they melt away.

—MANDINGO PROVERB

Truth shall prevail, and Freedom's light
  Shall speed its onward course,
Impeded by no human might . . .

—ADA, A YOUNG WOMAN OF COLOR

A man is a man, a woman is a woman, a child is a child, no matter where and these are the fundamental things, the inalienable things.

—JAMES BALDWIN

The simplest truths often meet the sternest resistance and are slowest in getting general acceptance.

—FREDERICK DOUGLASS

Unity

I don't know what to do. I know that something has to change in Birmingham. I don't know if I can raise money to get people out of jail. I do know I can go to jail with them. . . .

—MARTIN LUTHER KING, JR.

I n all things purely social we can be as separate as the five fingers, and yet one as the hand in all things essential to mutual progress.

—BOOKER T. WASHINGTON

W e cannot think of uniting with others, until after we have first united among ourselves. We cannot think of being acceptable to others until we have first proven acceptable to ourselves. One can't unite bananas with scattered leaves.

—MALCOLM X

*E*ven in our fractured state, all of us count and fit somewhere. We have proven that we can survive without each other. But we have not proven that we can win or make progress without each other. We must come together.

— JESSE JACKSON

*L*iberation is costly. It needs unity.

— DESMOND TUTU

*L*et nothing and nobody break your spirit. Let the unity in the community remain intact.

— JESSE JACKSON

*W*e can all sing together, but we can't all talk together.

— AFRICAN-AMERICAN PROVERB

Victory

Today we are building upon that legacy of struggle.

—JESSE JACKSON

For evil is strong and only with God can it be fought.

—ERNA BRODBER

The fight is not between black and white, woman against man, but between some people against some people.

—RED JORDAN AROBATEAU

If you have no confidence in self, you are twice defeated in the race of life. With confidence, you have won even before you have started.

—MARCUS GARVEY

F acing the rising sun of our new day begun,
Let us march on till victory is won.

— JAMES WELDON JOHNSON

I glory in conflict, that I may hereafter exult in victory.

— FREDERICK DOUGLASS

W hen I found I had crossed that line, I looked at my hands to see if I was the same person. There was such a glory over everything; the sun came like gold through the trees, and over the fields, and I felt like I was in Heaven.

— HARRIET TUBMAN

P eople don't pay much attention to you when you are second best. I wanted to see what it felt like to be number one.

— FLORENCE GRIFFITH JOYNER

Our time has come. Suffering breeds characters. Character breeds faith. And in the end, faith will not disappoint.

Our time has come. Our faith, hope and dreams will prevail. Our time has come. Weeping has endured for the night. And, now joy cometh in the morning.

Our time has come. No graves can hold our body down.

Our time has come. No lie can live forever.

Our time has come. We must leave racial battleground and come to economic common ground and moral higher ground. America, our time has come.

We've come from disgrace to Amazing Grace, our time has come.

—JESSE JACKSON

If you surrender to the wind, you can ride it.

—TONI MORRISON

Too many victories weaken you. The defeated can rise up stronger than the victor.

—MUHAMMAD ALI

Our real victory is not so much the desegregation of the buses as it is a new sense of dignity and destiny.

— MARTIN LUTHER KING, JR.

Life is to be lived, not controlled, and humanity is won by continuing to play in face of certain defeat.

— RALPH ELLISON

Mouth don't win the war. It don't even win the people. Neither does haste, urgency, and stretch-out-now insistence.

— TONI CADE BAMBARA

the terrible represents all that hinders, all that opposes human aspiration, and the marvelous represents the triumph of the human spirit over chaos. While the terms and conditions are different and often change, our triumphs are few and thus must be recognized for what they are and preserved.

— RALPH ELLISON

$\mathcal{V}$iolence

$\mathcal{N}$o justice, no peace.

— AL SHARPTON

$\mathcal{O}$rganizing is not gentle.

— W. E. B. DU BOIS

$\mathcal{V}$iolence seldom accomplishes permanent and desired results. Herein lies the futility of war.

— A. PHILIP RANDOLPH

$\mathcal{C}$ruelty is the strength of the wicked.

— MANDINGO PROVERB

I didn't want to hurt him more than I had to.

— JOE LOUIS

*T*he [boxing] ring was the only place a Negro could whip a white man and not be lynched.

— MALCOLM X

*I*t was all right to throw cinders. The greatest harm a cinder could do was leave a bruise. But broken bottles were dangerous; they left you cut, bleeding, and helpless.

— RICHARD WRIGHT

*W*hat does one say to his comrades at the moment when The Leader falls? All comment seems irrelevant. If the source of death is so-called natural causes, or an accident, the reaction is predictable, a feeling of impotence, humbleness, helplessness before the forces of the universe. But when the cause of death is an assassin's bullet, the overpowering desire is for vengeance.

— ELDRIDGE CLEAVER

... *t* he Negro has been constantly subjected to some form of organized violence ever since he became free.

— MARY CHURCH TERRELL

T he violent act is the desperate act. It is the imperious demand of a person to force another to honor his desire and need to be cared for, to be understood.

— HOWARD THURMAN

T he ultimate weakness of violence is that it is a descending spiral, begetting the very thing it seeks to destroy. Instead of diminishing evil, it multiplies it.

— MARTIN LUTHER KING, JR.

A word to the violent has never been sufficient
They have a hard speech that shatters conversation.

— RAYMOND PATTERSON

When a government decides to ban political organizations of the oppressed, intensifies oppression, and does not allow any free political activity, no matter how peaceful and nonviolent, then the people have no alternative but to resort to violence.

—NELSON MANDELA

Who makes you pay in tears, you make him pay in blood.

—MASAI PROVERB

They hit the streets in Watts not because Negroes like to drink or to steal, but because they've been in jail too long. Because a new law had been passed making fair housing illegal. Looting went on all right. What was not said was who stole from whom first. It's a great thing to be in Sacramento devising laws locking people into a ghetto. It's another thing to be locked in that ghetto.

—JAMES BALDWIN

We love only heroes. Glorious
death in battle. Scaling walls,
burning bridges behind us, destroying
all ways back. All retreat.

—LeRoi Jones (Amiri Baraka)

I'm so fast I could hit you before God gets the news.

—Muhammad Ali

Wisdom

It don't make much diffunce whar de rain comes fum, jes'
so it hits de groun' in de right place.

—from a slave narrative

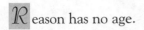

*R*eason has no age.

— AFRICAN PROVERB

*I*t is not the eye that understands but the mind.

— AFRICAN PROVERB

*E*very man got a right to his own mistakes. Ain't no man that ain't made any.

— JOE LOUIS

*T*here is always a person greater and lesser than yourself.

— ANONYMOUS

A man is born with all the wisdom he needs for life.

— DICK GREGORY

*A*ll human wisdom is summed up in two words, wait and hope.

— ALEXANDRE DUMAS

Wisdom is the gift, the endowments to know how to use power. Knowledge is only an instrument in the hand of wisdom.

— DANIEL PAYNE

Wisdom does not live in only one house.

— ASHANTI PROVERB

There are many forms of lunacy, but only one kind of common sense.

— IBO PROVERB

It is wise to let an offense repeat itself at least three times: the first offense may be an accident, the second a mistake, but the third is likely to be intentional.

— BOTSWANI PROVERB

You have three friends in this world: courage, sense, and wisdom.

— FON PROVERB

You can hide the smoke, but what you go' do with the fire?
— AFRICAN-AMERICAN PROVERB

... *i* f you see somebody winning all the time, he isn't gambling, he's cheating.

— MALCOLM X

Oh, I must search for wisdom every hour,
Deep in my wrathful bosom sore and raw,
And find in it the superhuman power
To hold me to the letter of your law!
Oh, I must keep my heart inviolate
Against the potent poison of your hate.

— CLAUDE MCKAY

The key to understanding others is to understand oneself.
— HELEN WILLIAMS

Women

I am glad to see that men are getting their rights, but I want women to get theirs, and while the water is stirring I will step into the pool.

— SOJOURNER TRUTH

N ow the fundamental agency under God in the regeneration, the re-training of the race, as well as the ground work and starting point of its progress upward, must be the black woman.

— ANNA J. COOPER

T hat I will be free to be who I will be, free to become whatever my life requires of me, without posturing, without compromise, without terror. That I will soon be able, realistically, to assume the dignified fulfillment of the dreams and needs and potentialities of most of the men, women, and children alive, today. That I can count upon a sisterhood and a brotherhood that will let me give my life to its consecration, without equivocating, without sorrow. That my son, who is a Black man, and that I, a Black woman, may keep faith with each other, and with those others whom we may have the privilege to serve, and to join.

— JUNE JORDAN

It is fallacious reasoning that in order for the Black man to be strong, the Black woman has to be weak.

— FRANCES BEALE

Our females must be qualified, because they are to be the mothers of our children. As mothers are the first nurses and instructors of children; from them children consequently, get their first impressions, which being always the most lasting, should be the most correct.

— MARTIN DELANY

And ain't I a woman? Look at me? Look at my arm! I have ploughed, and planted, and gathered into barns, and no man could head me! And ain't I a woman? I could work as much and eat as much as a man—when I could get it—and bear the lash as well! And ain't I a woman? I have borne thirteen children, and seen 'em mos' all sold off to slavery, and when I cried out with my mother's grief, none but Jesus heard me! And ain't I a woman?

—SOJOURNER TRUTH

No golden weights can turn the scale
　　Of justice in His sight;
And what is wrong in woman's life
　　In man's cannot be right.

—FRANCES ELLEN WATKINS HARPER

The old, subjective, stagnant, indolent and wretched life for woman has gone. She has as many resources as men, as many activities beckon her on. As large possibilities swell and inspire her heart.

—ANNA J. COOPER

*N*othing lies nearer the heart of colored women than children.

—MARY CHURCH TERRELL

I am convinced that the black man will only reach his full potential when he learns to draw upon the strengths and insights of the black woman.

—MANNING MARABLE

*B*y coming into close touch with the masses of our women it is possible to correct many of the evils which militate so seriously against us and inaugurate the reforms, without which, as a race, we cannot hope to succeed.

—MARY CHURCH TERRELL

*T*he true worth of a race must be measured by the character of its womanhood. . . .

—MARY MCLEOD BETHUNE

I AM A BLACK WOMAN

I am a black woman
the music of my song
some sweet arpeggio of tears
is written in a minor key
and I
can be heard humming in the night
Can be heard
        humming
in the night

—MARI EVANS

*W*e, the black women of today, must accept the full weight of a legacy wrought in blood by our mothers in chains. As heirs of a tradition of perseverance and heroic resistance, we must hasten to take our place wherever our people are forging toward freedom.

—ANGELA YVONNE DAVIS

*W*oman, if the soul of the nation is to be saved, I believe that you must become its soul.

—CORETTA SCOTT KING

When sweetness becomes excessive, it is no longer sweetness.

— LUBA PROVERB

Woman can whisper her cruel wrongs into the ear of a very dear friend much easier than she can record them for the world to read.

— HARRIET JACOBS

If the first woman God ever made was strong enough to turn the world upside down, all alone, together women ought to be able to turn it rightside up again.

— SOJOURNER TRUTH

get back fat black woman be a mother
grandmother strong thing but not woman

— NIKKI GIOVANNI

We are still, most of us, the Black woman who had to be almost frighteningly strong in order for us all to survive. For . . . she was the one whom they left . . . with the children to raise, who had to make it somehow or other. And we are still, so many of us, living that history.

—PAULE MARSHALL

There is one unalterable fact that too many of our men cannot seem to face. And that is, we "black, evil, ugly" women are a perfect and accurate reflection of you "black, evil, ugly" men. Play hide and seek as long as you can and will, but your every rejection and abandonment of us is only a sorry testament of how thoroughly and carefully you have been blinded and brainwashed. And let it further be understood that when we refer to you we mean, ultimately, us. For you are us, and vice versa.

—ABBEY LINCOLN

. . . there are any number of women around willing to walk ten paces back to give him the illusion of walking ten paces ahead.

—TONI CADE BAMBARA

*M*en have got to develop some heart and some sound analysis to realize that when sisters get passionate about themselves and their direction, it does not mean they're readying up to kick men's ass. They're readying up for honesty.

— TONI CADE BAMBARA

*A*in't nothin happened to you, ain't happened to most women whether they care to admit it or not. You strong, Babygirl. You a woman. You gotta be.

— MARILYN FULLEN-COLLINS

I feel that if I have to answer for the deeds done in my body just as much as a man, I have a right to have just as much as a man.

— SOJOURNER TRUTH

I was missing you
remember hips that used to call to me
lips that stopped my heart
swelled my womanness to overflowing

— FOLISADE

The women in my family have spent so much time consoling others, being brave, neglecting their own needs, being *strong black women*.

— TIYE MILAN SELAH

The sisters were my friends, not a "posse"; we met on the fly and compared notes, too busy for "hen parties" and "sisterfests." But none of us pretended we had more than a clue to how you hold the future; all of us out there scuffling, trying to be what the future said we could be: beautiful, successful, secure. We would be loved and valued as the brothers said our mothers had not been. But nothing had been promised to us and we didn't even have that to lose.

— SHERLEY ANNE WILLIAMS

a good girl always says yes
please and thank-you
she never takes chances with her self respect
or the impressions of others
she grows
with freedom of her imagination
as silent partner
she really lives in her head

— IMANI CONSTANCE JOHNSON-BURNETT

The young woman-smell
Of your poppy body
Rises to my brain as opium
Yet silently motionless
I sit with twitching fingers
Yea, even reverently
Sit I
With you and the blossoming night
For what flower, plucked,
Lingers long?

—FRANK MARSHALL DAVIS

Oh, little brown girl, born for sorrow's mate,
Keep all you have of queenliness,
Forgetting that you once were slave,
And let your full lips laugh at Fate!

—GWENDOLYN BENNETT

Abortions will not let you forget.
You remember the children you got that you did not get . . .

I have heard in the voices of the wind the voices of my dim
    killed children.
I have contracted. I have eased
My dim dears at the breasts they could never suck.

—GWENDOLYN BROOKS

There is a great stir about colored men getting their rights, but not a word about colored women; and if colored men get their rights, and not colored women theirs, you see, the colored men will be masters over the women and it will be as bad as before. So I am for keeping the thing going while things are stirring, because if we wait till it is still, it will take a great while to get it going again.

—SOJOURNER TRUTH

True chivalry respects all womanhood.

—IDA B. WELLS

Youth

Youth are looking for something; it's up to adults to show them what is worth emulating.

—JESSE JACKSON

When I was nineteen, I know I didn't know too much about what's goin' on. Except you s'posed to fight for your country. And you come home. But where is my country when I come home?

— SGT. ROBERT L. DANIELS, RADIO WIREMAN,
HOWITZER GUNNER

We were on top again. As always, again. We survived. The depths had been icy and dark, but now a bright sun spoke to our souls. I was no longer simply a member of the proud graduating class of 1940; I was a proud member of the wonderful, beautiful Negro race.

— MAYA ANGELOU

Youth never despairs, for it is still in harmony with the Divine.

— ALEXANDRE DUMAS

We will die without our young people.

— ALEX HALEY

Youth is the turning point in life, the most sensitive and volatile period, the state that registers most vividly the impressions and experience of life.

—RICHARD WRIGHT

When I was young and loved life's laughter,
I climbed tall hills and touched the sun;
I did not know till long years after
That ecstasy and pain are one.

—NAOMI LONG MADGETT

You are young, gifted, and Black. We must begin to tell our young, There's a world waiting for you, Yours is the quest that's just begun.

—JAMES WELDON JOHNSON

I am a mean hungry sorehead.
Do I have the capacity for grace?
to arise one smoking spring
& find one's youth has taken off
for greener parts.

—LEROI JONES (AMIRI BARAKA)

The young are not likely to follow the example of past generations who were radical in their teens, liberal in their twenties, conservative in their thirties and reactionary in their forties.

— WHITNEY YOUNG, JR.

If we can reach young people's minds deep enough, we can teach young minds deep enough so that they will change the negative concept they have of themselves from which most of the negative social consequences flow.

— OSSIE DAVIS

May those, whose holy task it is,
To guide impulsive youth,
Fail not to cherish in their souls
A reverence for truth . . .

— CHARLOTTE FORTEN [GRIMKÉ]

I ndex of $\mathcal{N}$ ames

$\mathcal{A}$cknowledgments

This book would not have been possible without Betsy Ryan, president of Bascom Communications. I am grateful also to Bill Thompson, the Rev. Mary Ann Williams, my mother, Margaret Johnson, and Helen Murtaugh; and for the intelligence and care given by Bob Bender and Johanna Li, two of Simon & Schuster's most valuable assets.